# THE
# PERILS
# OF
# AMATEUR STRATEGY

BULKINGTON BOOKS

# THE
# PERILS
# OF
# AMATEUR STRATEGY

## AS EXEMPLIFIED BY THE ATTACK ON THE
## DARDANELLES FORTRESS IN 1915

*BY*

*LIEUTENANT-GENERAL*

*SIR GERALD ELLISON, K.C.B., K.C.M.G.*

*late Headquarters Staff of the*

*Mediterranean Expeditionary Force, 1915*

*WITH A PREFATORY NOTE BY*

*THE RIGHT HON. VISCOUNT ESHER, G.C.B., G.C.V.O.*

"The English Generals are wanting in strategy.

We should have no chance if they possessed as much science as their officers and men had of courage and bravery.

They are lions led by donkeys."
General Ludendorff

*To the memory of the gallant men from all parts of the Empire who died during the Dardanelles–Gallipoli campaign in 1915, this volume is dedicated.*

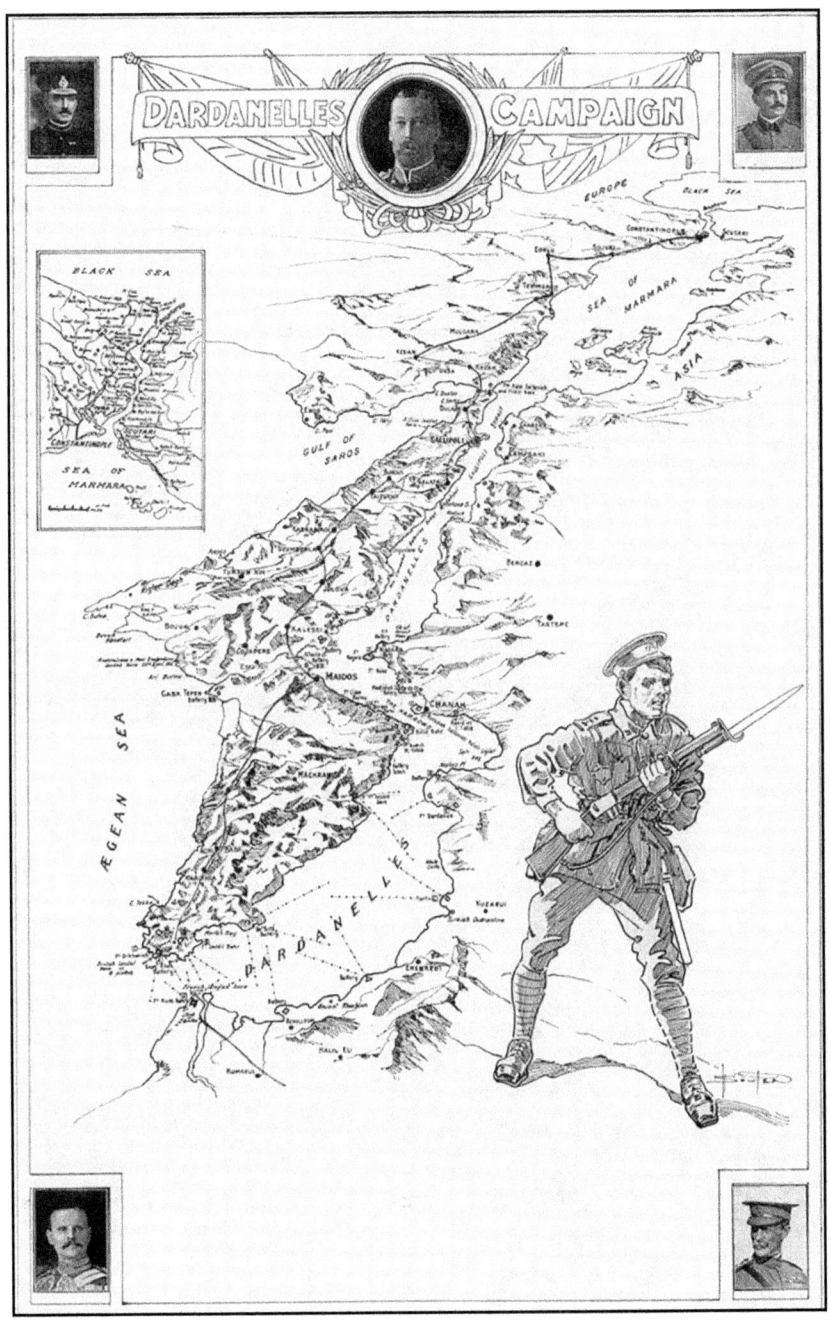

## New Publisher's Note

Blessed beloved bookreader, you have found this volume in your vision. We hope you read on, but let us offer a few humble words. Of making many books there is no end, and a long preface is a chasing after wind. We pray you give us a moment's indulgence.

Our mission is to build a bridge into the past, before film, television, copyright, and internet swallowed up the world. Before 'content' was culture. If the reader finds friends from before the echo chamber, they may find armor and sword against the dreadful noise machine.

We are convinced that many authors and many books are ready to rise like Lazarus and reenter the world to remind the readers that their life has purpose; that their time should be valued; and their history is an honorable home.

This book was chosen because it is a narrowly focused study on a technical matter—military strategy—that has great relevance today. We see an abundance of armchair generals and bloated top heavy organizations, and sub-optimal performances in many theatres of conflict.

We believe that the lessons of this book are quite clear and applicable to many situations today. We know you will enjoy it.

*Your Most Humble and Obedient Servant (YMHOS),*

*Arthur Bulkington,*

*Melville Bay*

*The Perils Of*

# Publisher's Foreword

This book is assuredly a piece of "inside baseball." It is written by a decorated General, and aimed primarily at the upper echelons of the British military and political elites of its time. It is not a first hand account of Gallipoli, though he served there, or a general history of the campaign, though he could write one, or a hagiography of the bravery of the ANZAC lads, who he honored. It is a genre of book that is quite rare nowadays. It is an angry man telling the truth. It is an act of retribution. It is a jeremiad against dysfunctional military bureaucracy that cost the lives of good men.

We will note here that he is especially agitated about the actions of Mr. Winston Churchill, who he believes was a key personality that led to the mismanagement of the theatre of operations. In the preface written at the time, Lord Esher notices this same point, while disagreeing with the author.

Nearly a century later, in 2025, when this book is being re-issued, there has been the beginning of a historiographical reappraisal of Mr. Winston Churchill. We believe that this is one reason we should re-issue this book, because that debate is only beginning, and the facts presented by General Ellison are relevant.

But that is not the only reason. As ever, we wish to spell out to you, the Reader, why this short book is worth your time.

As we conceive it, the duty of a foreword is to make three points.
1) Why we liked it. Why it was worth our time.
2) Why it has relevance today.
3) Why it is worth your precious reading time.

Picking up on the first thing we said, it's "inside baseball." It is a niche subject written by a subject matter expert for his fellow experts. In this case, a decorated career soldier, writing for his fellow top brass and diplomats.

He saw lives wasted, and ships sunk from bad decisions made by the highest circles. He sincerely believes the Gallipoli operation was mismanaged. He points to other plans that could have been a better use of resources and shortened the war. He also describes how the Gallipoli operation could have been better planned and coordinated. He can name names and point to specific meetings where wrong choices were made.

What comes out of this is something you won't necessarily find in most books on grand strategy, how much 'personnel is policy.' That fact is obfuscated for many reasons. Not least of which is, as we see here, the erasure of personal culpability in choices that send thousands of men to their death.  Far better to hide behind concepts like 'containment' or 'rapprochement' or 'fighting for freedom', and then let later historians write off these preventable and pointless deaths with handwavings about 'glory' or 'intelligence failures.'

Such a book, precisely because of its narrow focus on one campaign, and on the upper echelons of decisionmaking, is a perfect microcosm. As the author says, *ex pede Herculem!* from the foot of Hercules we can calculate his entirety.

For our part, we found it enormously insightful. We also began to see Winston Churchill in a new light. General Ellison shows, at several points, where he was wrong, and where he manipulated outcomes, and where he broke traditional customs and chain of command. General Ellison, like Patton facing off Rommel, carefully read his opponent's book, *World In Crisis* to pull out all the discrepancies and mythmaking. We once admired Churchill greatly, as most men of our age did, but have come to see room for an entirely different interpretation. One worth considering. For this we are grateful, and enjoyed our time working on this manuscript.

Now, how could such a niche book be relevant today? Where in our world today do we see myopic bureaucratic organizations focused on individual careerism instead of strategic victory?

To name a few military issues that come to mind:

In 2021, the American withdrawal from Afghanistan reached

its final stage. They chose to abandon Bagram Air Force Base and continue the withdrawal from Kabul airport. They left immense amounts of equipment, vehicles, and supplies behind. This was a very foolish tactical choice, and made evacuation harder and cost more lives. This was obvious to many outside observers.

In 2023, there was a much vaunted 'summer counter-offensive' that Ukraine was going to launch and change the calculus of the conflict. This required more foreign money and equipment. It got alot of press coverage in the buildup. Outside observers predicted this would not work. The reasons were obvious, manpower, training, geography. And it did not.

From these bad decisions, we can calculate the entirety of the competence of the larger military decisonmaking process.

We could probably also find ways to apply this book's insights to businesses and organizations. Rule-by-Committee is a besetting evil in industry and entertainment and elsewhere.

General Ellison makes his point that "war is too important to be left to the politicians," contra M. Clemenceau. We have to concede that this argument carries weight in light of Gallipoli, the fall of Kabul, and the Ukrainian counter-offensive.

As to our last point, why it's worth the Reader's precious time, we do not pretend this book is for everyone. In point of fact, only certain kinds of people could benefit from re-litigating Gallipoli, and re-evaluating Winston Churchill. Those kinds of people know themselves, and will find this book if they are meant to. But these kinds of people are the leading edge of culture and help form the opinions and consensus of millions, and give birth to new possibilities. They are professional military men, diplomats, and the amateur historians and political vanguards, the Sensitive Young Men of a certain slice of the internet.

Our hope is it finds young readers and awakens in them a desire to build great fleets and command powerful ships, to serve honorably and well, and to stand tall against politicians who muddle the chain of command and doom men to pointless deaths.

*Your Most Humble and Obedient Servant (YMHOS),*
*Arthur Bulkington,*
*Melville Bay*

MAJ.-GEN. SIR G. F. ELLISON, K.C.M.G.     *F. A. Swaine phot.*

*General Ellison, preparing winter quarters, in Gallipoli, 1915-1916.*

## Contemporary News Clippings

*Reading Eagle*

*November 13, 1915*

*Will Explain His Dramatic Exit*

*Churchill, Former Member of Cabinet, to Fight with British Army in France*

London, November 13th, 3:05 A.M.—Winston Spencer Churchill, formerly first lord of the admiralty, whose retirement from the Cabinet as chancellor of the duchy of Lancaster was officially announced last night, intends to explain the reason for his resignation at the sitting of the House of Commons on Monday. According to the *Times'* Parliamentary Correspondent, Mr. Churchill will review the war operations of the admiralty during his term as first lord and will justify the expeditions to Antwerp and the Dardanelles.

The Times takes the view that, although Mr. Churchill's action recalls the equally dramatic resignation of his father, it is not likely to close his political career as it did in his father's case.

"Mr. Churchill's great gifts and vivid imagination," the newspaper says, "have been amply demonstrated in his dread of office, and there are few who would venture to predict his permanent withdrawal from public life."

He will now join the British army in France and take an active part in the fight against the Teutonic allies.

### Severely Criticised

No figure in British politics has been the target for more criticism since the war started than Winston Spencer Churchill.

Mr. Churchill assumed the least important position in the Cabinet, that of the chancellorship of the duchy of Lancaster, when the coalition ministry was formed last May after having held the important post of the first lord of the admiralty. Incidentally Mr. Churchill's change of office did not reduce the flood of criticism which starts as a rule from public statements which older men call, at least, indiscreet. He will be 41 years old Nov. 30, but according to his critics, he does not acquire discretion with years.

Rightly or wrongly, Churchill has been blamed as if solely responsible for the inadequacy of the British relief of Antwerp, a military movement that brought little relief to the Belgians and ende with the interment of a large part of the British marine expedition in Holland. Similarly he has had the brunt of the public censure for attempting to force the Dardanelles without the help of the army, a failure which has up to date produced a British casualty list of approximately 100,000 men. It is logically unreasonable to place upon his young shoulders the responsibility for both of these undertakings which could not have been made without the approval of his older Cabinet associates, but public criticism is least of all things logical, and he is termed with unrelenting criticism "The Duke of Antwerp and Gallipoli"

## *His Boastful Manners*

Possibly he would not thus be forced to bear the full brunt of this disapproval if he were not addicted to a rather boastful or over-confident method of public address. His prophecy early in the war that if German ships did not come out and fight, "We would dig them out of their holes like rats," his prediction that if Zeppelins came to England they would be surrouned by "a swarm of hornets" and his claim of Dundee, where he went to speak before his constituency after his clash with Admiral Fisher, that the British on the Gallipoli Peninsula were "within a few miles" of a great victory, are typical instances of this form of oratory.

One of the comic weeklines, poking fun at Churchill's recently adopted avocation of painting, pictures him with easel and palette before canvases depicting rats in holes and swarms of hornets and titles its cartoon:

"A promising painter, somewhat lacking in execution."

On Trafalgar day, he made another mistake, according to his critics when he wrote "through our long delays the enemy has seized a new initiative in the near east." One day when he was present in the House of Commons he was asked "how the delays had arisen and who had been responsible for them." Not long before he had been chatting with David Lloyd George on the treasury bench, but when the question was put he had disappeared. Cheers greeted the question and members called out "He was here: he is in the House," and Mr. Hogge, one of the prominent baiters asked "Why has he run away?"

Several days later he expressed regret that he was not present when the question was asked, saying he meant that the delay was incidental to the joint action in military and diplomatic affairs of the various allied governments among whom the responsibility was shared.

*The Perils Of*
## Ottawa Citizen

## May 13, 1915

## British Sub. "E-14" Through Dardanelles; H.M.S. Goliath Sunk in a Torpedo Attack

### 500 Lost on Battleship; E14 Sinks Three Turkish Boats in Sea of Marmora

### Mr. Churchill Announces Loss of Predreadnought and Submarine's Daring Exploit. Progress in Naval Land Operations Strengthens Belief Early Fall of Great Dardanelles Barrier. Enveloping Gallipoli.

London, May 13th.—(3 P.M.)

The British battleship Goliath has been torpedoed in the Dardanelles. Twenty Officers and 160 men of the crew were saved.

Announcement of the loss of the *Goliath* was made in the house of commons this afternoon by Winston Spencer Churchill, first lord of the admiralty. While no definite information apparently had then been received as to the number of lives lost, Mr. Churchill said he feared it would reach 500.

### E-14 Passes Dardanelles

Mr. Churchill also announced that the British submarine E-14 had penetrated through the Dardanelles and into the sea of Marmara, sinking two Turkish gunboats and a Turkish transport.

### How Goliath Was Lost

Mr. Churchill, on announcing the loss of the *Goliath* said: "The *Goliath* was torpedoed last night during a torpedo attack by destroyers while protecting the French flank just inside the straits.

"Twenty officers and 160 men were saved, which I fear means that over 500 were lost."

### The E-14 Exploit

"The admiral commanding at the Dardanelles also telegraphs that the submarine E-14, which, with so much daring, penetrated to the sea of Marmora, has reported that she sank two Turkish gunboats and a large Turkish transport."

The Goliath was built at Chatham, England, completed in 1900. She was of 12,950 tons displacement and carried a crew of 750. She was 400 feet long on the water line and 74 feet beam. Her armament consisted of four 12-inch, twelve 6-inch guns and 20 smaller guns as well as four submerged 18-inch torpedo tubes. She was a sister ship to the *Canopus* of Falkland Island fame and of the *Ocean,* sunk a month ago in an assault on the Dardanelles forts. The Goliath was one of the 15-year-old predreadnought battleships, very useful for the work in hand at the Dardanelles. Britain has plenty of such vessels.

The E-14 is one of the very latest of the British submarines and fully up to the best the Germans have, both in speed and efficiency.

## Enveloping The Peninsula

London, May 13.—London was cheered today by the publication of a despatch from Athens recording a decided advance of the British and French troops along the Gallipoli peninsula. Some reports even claimed the occupation of certain heights which would mean the entire peninsula was under the control of the invaders.

## Great Work by Fleet

Paris, May 13.—A Havas despatch from Athens says:

"An allied fleet re-entered the Dardanelles last night and bombarded the forts of Kilid Bahr, Chanak Kalessi and Nagara. The bombardment was interrupted at eight o'clock but was resumed three hours later and is being continued.

"Although the Turks have been strongly reinforced the bombardment from allied warships is causing them heavy losses, and they are steadily losing ground. Turkish trenches are filled with bodies."

## Making Steady Progress

Mitylene, May 12. (Special to *Daily Telegraph*, London.)—Considerable progress has been made by the allies since a week ago, when they had advanced four miles up the Gallipoli Peninsula. The position three days ago was that the Turks were fighting desperately to prevent their being pushed into the sea between Maidos and the town of Gallipoli. The allied troops from Sedd-el-Barh, Gabtene, and the Gulf of Saros were coverging on them assisted by the fire of the ships on both sides.

## Warship Fire

From the Gulf of Saros the Queen Elizabeth and other warships were concentrating a heavy fire on Plaiar and the north end of the Bulair lines to prevent the Turks from crossing to Gallipoli to join the forces near the town. Gallipoli was in flames as a result of the bombardment of the fleet.

It is evident that hard fighting must be expected between Maidos and Gallipoli as the Turks have greatly strengthened the fortifications since the first attack on the Dardanelles. They have lines of trenches about 30 meters apart and artillery on the surrounding heights.

## Abuse of White Flag

When the British, advancing from the neighborhood of Yeni Kei, and the French from Gaba Tepe, were converging on the Turks the latter showed a white flag, shouting to British and French:

"We are friends. Don't fire."

The British and French ceased firing only to be met at close quarters with a hail of shrapnel. Very fierce fighting followed and both sides suffered heavy losses. The Turks are now being driven toward the sea. Turkish prisoners state that they would have retreated but the Germans behind them with revolvers shot them if they attempted to do so. They express the belief that it is impossible for their German masters to withstand the allies' advance.

## Evening Tribune

## January 10, 1916

### Allied Troops Abandon All Gallipoli Positions

#### Evacuation Effected Without the Loss of a Man is Declared in British Official Statement — One Soldier Wounded

London, January 10th.—The remaining positions held by the allies on Gallipoli Peninsula have now been abandoned with the wounding of only one man among the British and French, according to a British official statement issued to-night.

This news has been expected for several days by the keener observers of the near eastern campaign, for the retirement of the troops from Anzac and Suvla Bay three weeks ago left no strategic advantage to the retention of the tip of the peninsula. Nevertheless, the news will be received with regret by the people of the British Isles, as well as the colonies.

Renewed activity of various kinds noted by the Turkish official communications in the past few days has presumably been in the nature of preparations for the final act of the Dardanelles tragedy. To-night's Turkish official, covering the period from Thursday to Saturday, records increasing effectiveness of the reinforced Turkish batteries, which have been drawing in and concentrating on the allies' remaining positions.

Gen. Charles Monro, according to the British official statement, reports that only one British soldier was wounded in the official evacuation of the Gallipoli peninsula, that there were no casualties among the French and that all the guns were saved, except 17 worn out ones which were blown up.

The official communications issued last evening says:

"Gen. Sir Monro reports the complete evacuation of Gallipoli has been successfully carried out."

"All the guns and howitzers were got away, with the exception of 17 worn out guns, which were blown up by us before leaving."

"Our casualties amounted to one member of the British rank and file wounded."

"There were no casualties among the French."

"Gen. Monro states that the accomplishment of this difficult task was due to Gens. Birdwood and Davis and invaluable assistance rendered in an operation of the highest difficulty by Admiral De Robeck and the royal navy."

## Violent Battle, Says Turks

The British as a result of a violent battle have completely evacuated Seddul Bahr, with great losses, says a great dispatch to Amsterdam from Constantinople. Not a single man remained behind.

The dispatch adds that newspaper reports from the Dardanelles say the Turks have completely driven the French and British from Seddul Bahr, and that Gallipoli peninsula "is now clear of the enemy."

Effective work by Turkish artillery is bombarding the allied positions on the Gallipoli peninsula is reported in the Turkish official statement issued to-day by the War Office. The statement says:

"On the Dardanelles front Thursday night there was rather brisk bomb fighting on our right and left wings. On Friday our artillery for some hours at intervals violently shelled hostile trenches opposite our right wing, causing heavy damage. In the centre our artillery and our bombs destroyed some hostile trenches and bomb and mortar positions. On our left wing there was a feeble artillery duel. Two cruisers, a monitor and four torpedo craft assisted the enemy's land batteries."

"At 3 o'clock in the afternoon our shells caused an outbreak of fire in the enemy's camp near Teke Burnu."

"On the night of Thursday our batteries in the narrows effectively shelled the enemy's camp near Seddul Bahr, and on Friday the enemy's batteries in the region of Teke Burnu. The enemy's Seddul Bahr batteries and a cruiser and a monitor anchored near Teke Burnu replied unsuccessfully. On Saturday our Anatolian batteries effectively shelled the harbors at Seddul Bahr and Teke Burnu."

"A group of hostile troops is in the valleys near Kere Vizzere and Mortoliman."

# The Sydney Herald

## January 5, 1933

## Sir Ian Hamilton

## Gallipoli Criticisms

## "This Senseless Evacuation."

London, December 1st.—Australians in London were immensely intrigued by the publication of a lecture by General Sir Ian Hamilton, who, when speaking to the British Legion at Birkenhead, made a remarkable attack on certain wartime politicians, generals, and admirals, and described the evacuation of Gallipoli as "senseless." He denounced the Cabinet Dardanelles Committee in almost sensational terms, characterising it as "the worst war directorate the world has seen, with the exception of Antony and Cleopatra—and they had at least the excuse of love, which cannot be urged for Mr. Asquith and Mr. Lloyd George." As the withdrawal of the Anzac, British, and French troops from the Peninsula, there was no question of them being driven off: the responsibility rested solely with politicians, an "ineffective" War Office, and some senior officers, "at home and at the front, who, personally fearless, began to tremble for their beloved ships as soon as they saw a fort." "When Nelson saw a fort," said Sir Ian, "he began to tremble—not for his ships, but for the fort. We did possess at the Dardanelles the very spit and spirit of Nelson, who felt exactly like Nelson felt, and who, if he had been given the task, would have take the fleet slap through the Narrows within a week—Sir Roger Keyes, a leader somewhat hasty for the creepy crawly ways of peace, but for war without a peer."

Strongly criticising the setting up by Mr. Asquith of the "Dardanelles-Committee-cum-Cabinet." Sir Ian Hamilton declared that he had never been able to conjecture what suicidal impulse, or what enemy in the mask of a friend, could have prompted Mr. Asquith to institute that boomerang commission. If it was meant to make the scapegoat generals into mincemeat, said Sir Ian, it would be funny it if turned out to have stewed their statesmen in their own juice, and canned them into mock turtle soup for posterity.

There were two or three happenings which gave him the impression that strings were being pulled behind Mr. Asquith's back. Mr. Asquith was as straight as a die, but someone was not, "and unless I flash back a searchlight now, the happenings will disappear for ever, which would not be quite fair on the historian."

Sir Ian took Mr. Lloyd George to task for asserting in an interview that "we had been driven out of Gallipoli." "Mr. Lloyd George will not doubt stick to his guns," he said, "and what is more, I am sure that he, if any man, can explain how it came about that we 'had been driven out of Gallipoli' As for me, it is my duty to point out that the troops I knew so well were never driven out by the enemy. All the Germans and Turks who could possibly have been concentrated and fed upon that peninsula could never have driven us out."

## Fixing the Blame

"To me this senseless evacuation seemed as big a moment in the world history as has ever taken place since the Greeks evacuated Troy and pretended to sail away homeward, leaving the Wooden Horse behind them. We, alas! made no pretence: left no wooden horse behind us; only the dead bodies still warm of 500 mules shot at the last moment to save them from being led in triumph through the streets of Constantinople."

Dealing with the story—still heard in some quarters—of now General Sir Stanley Maude, commander of the 13th Division, remained on the Peninsula 20 minutes after the last troops had gone, "because he had lost his valise," Sir Ian Hamilton said he had good reason to believe this was not the correct explanation. "For me," said Sir Ian, "I prefer to believe, and I have reason for doing so, that Maude did not wait 20 minutes after everyone else, with a rising storm threatening his life, for the sake of a valise, but that he wished to close the Dardanelles evacuation with a superb gesture of protest and disdain."

Sir Ian, discussing why the evacuation was carried out, said: "First and foremost I blame myself for things having gone so wrong, but not for my tactical plans or military orders. These have by now run the gauntlet of examinations by experts, home and foreign and still stand upon their legs."

"No, but because I so culpably neglected the ceaseless internecine war raging on the Home Front of Whitehall and Fleet-Street. Secondly, because we had no effective General Staff at the War Office to weigh impartially the values of the various theatres and to distribute support accordingly. Thirdly, because of the undue influence under these conditions of G.H.Q. in France, plus the Government of France and it's C.Q.G. Fourthly, because of an inferiority complex on the part of senior naval officers at home and at the front who, personally fearless as they were, began to tremble for their beloved ships as soon as they saw a fort."

Never one to mince his words, General Sir Ian Hamilton evidently spoke of many things that had been rankling in his heart for years. His lecture made a deep impression on the popular mind, which has never yet been able to grasp "the truth behind Gallipoli." Australians who took part in the Peninsular campaign will at all events agree with his declaration that the evacuation was not caused by any threat of being "driven off," even though the prospect of making further progress was unpromising, having regard to the troops and armament available. The evacuation was as deep a mystery to them at the time as it has remained to most people ever since, whether it was "senseless" or otherwise.

# MAPS

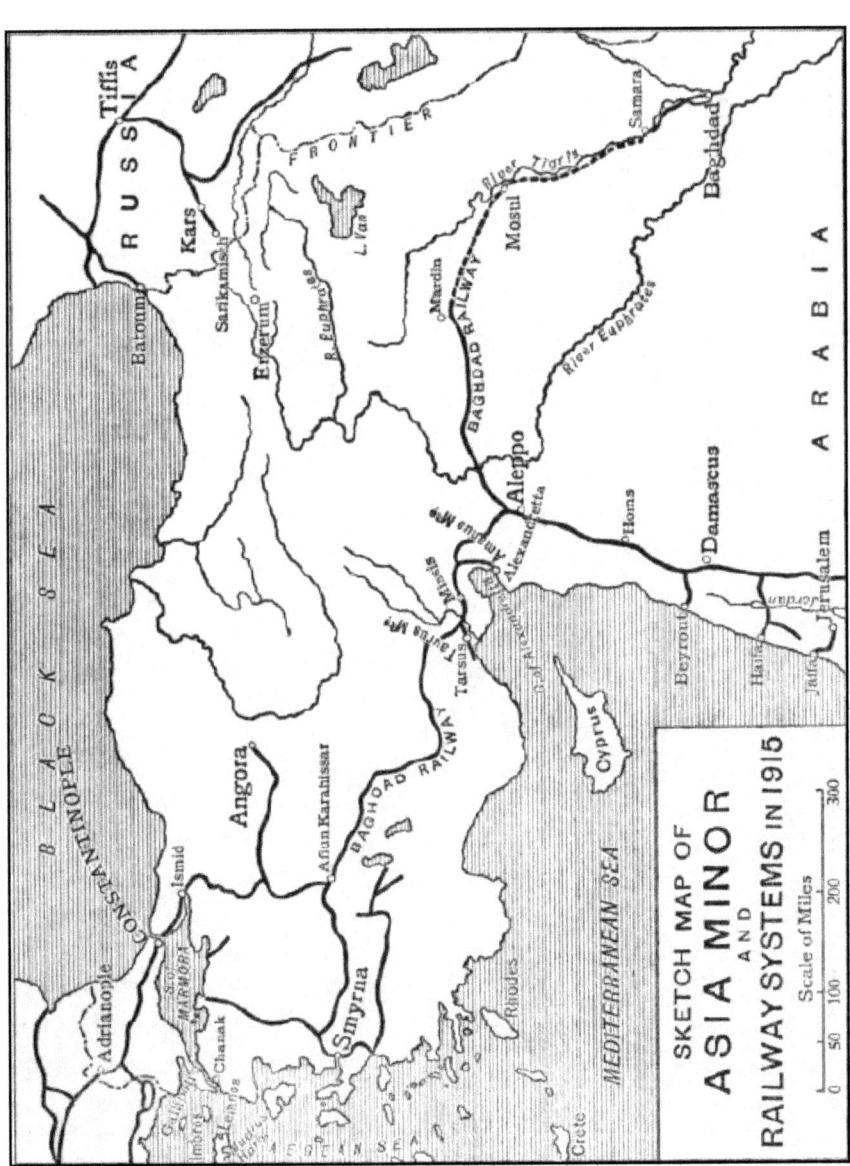

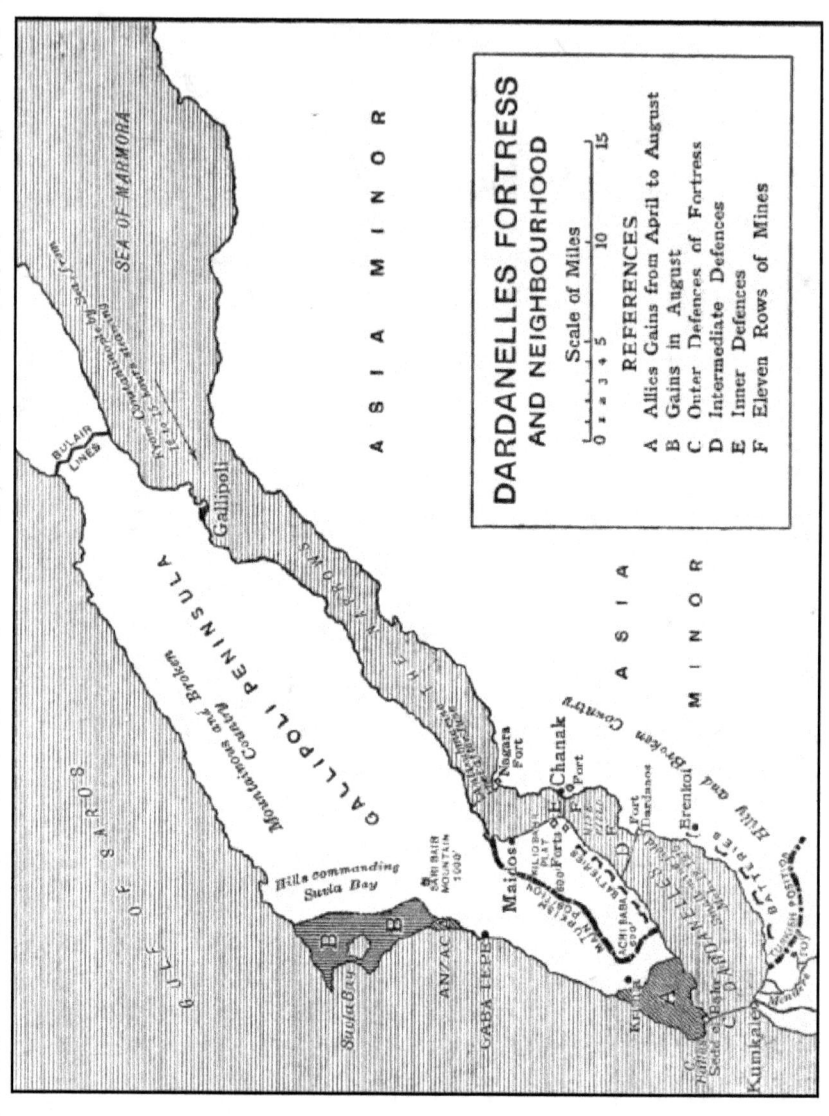

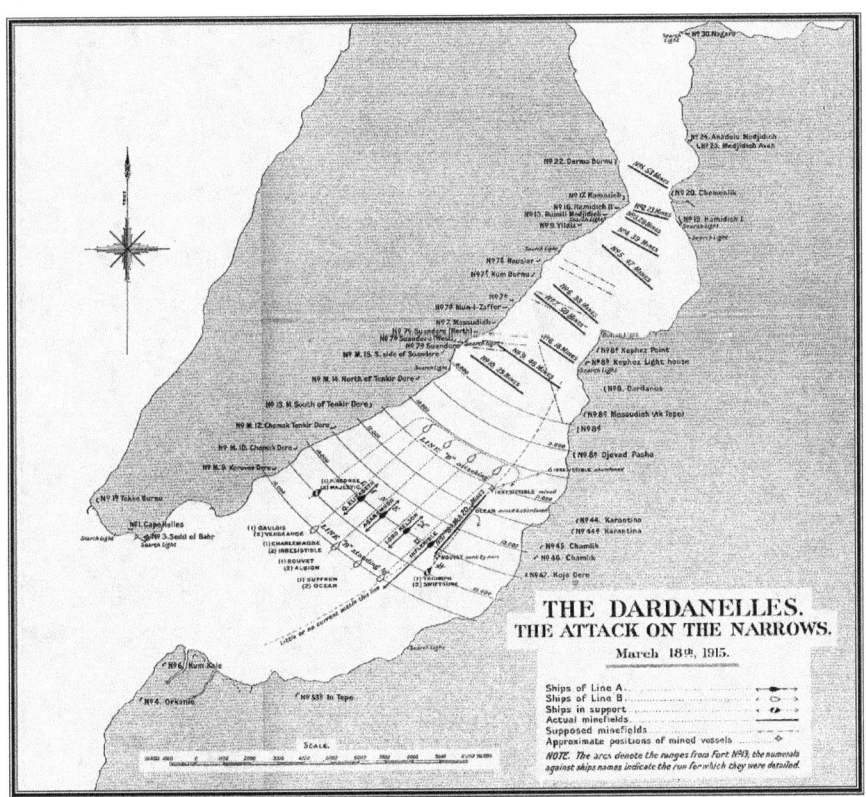

THE DARDANELLES.
THE ATTACK ON THE NARROWS.
March 18th, 1915.

# Contents

# PREFATORY NOTE

## *BY THE RT. HON. VISCOUNT ESHER, G.C.B., G.C.V.O.*[1]

I cannot refuse Sir Gerald Ellison, who was Secretary to our War Office Reconstitution Committee, and who kept us all straight, the request that he has made me to read his book and write a few words of preface.

Although I do not agree with much of his argument, I sympathise with his broad conclusions. Perhaps it was impossible to write such a book—and it was well worth writing, and still better worth publishing just now—without severely handling politicians, seamen, and soldiers, who were forced by circumstances to conduct a great war under impossible conditions.

General Ellison does not believe politicians to be capable of dealing with naval and military strategy. He admits that among self-governing peoples, statesmen, responsible and selected, must settle questions of war and peace. But he seems to see his way, at some undetermined moment, to hand over the strategy of war to "professionals"! The transition moment is so difficult to fix, the strands of military and civil life are so intertwined, that his problem appears to me insoluble.

Nor can I agree with his strictures on Mr. Churchill. In war it is precisely the temperament of Mr. Churchill that is wanted in a leader or a commander. General Ellison must forgive me for saying that the civilian Chatham, whom he selects for high praise, was just such another. A "cornet of horse"—like Mr. Churchill, and like him of fiery, impetuous temper. But Chatham had a free hand and amazing good fortune, while Mr. Churchill had neither.

The word "amateur" that General Ellison uses is misleading. You cannot rule out the "amateur" when you come to the governing of

---

1    Publisher's Note (most footnotes are originally by the author, and when appropriate, we will add our footnotes going forward with the mark "P.N." to distinguish our additions to the originals): Reginald Baliol Bretty, 2nd Viscount Esher (1852-1930), was a historian and liberal M.P. He backed the Jameson raid, and investigated the British Army's mistakes in the Boer War. He worked as an emissary to France in the First World War, and after the war he helped enact further modernizations of the British military.

States, the direction of armies, the carrying forward of great enterprises. From Clive to Kitchener, the provinces and dominions of the British Empire are strewn with "amateurs"— that is to say, men whose genius triumphed over their lack of expert training. Therefore, while disagreeing with General Ellison's main argument by which he reaches his perfectly sound conclusion, I must admit that he has illustrated it with personal experience and knowledge of the Great War in a manner better calculated than most other books on the war to draw attention to the weakness of our naval and military system, and to suggest a remedy.

The Committee which bears my name reorganised, with General Ellison's assistance, the Defence Committee, and created a General Staff, basing the organisation of the Army in times of peace upon its functions in times of war. But we failed to foresee that when war broke out the Defence Committee would be swept away altogether, and that the General Staff would be merged in the active command of our armies in the field.

Yet that is what happened. I do not pretend that anything else could have been done under a system, sound in itself, that was never properly put into operation. In August 1914 everybody believed, in spite of the Russo-Japanese War, in spite of warnings from students of modern tactics both on sea and land, that another Trafalgar was imminent, and that Sir John French would gallop over the frontiers of Germany at the head of a mobile force. Every General Staff officer wanted, quite naturally, to be "in the show," and London, which was nearer to the Ypres salient than Versailles was to Verdun, was thought to be a backwater.

General Ellison refers to Anson and Ligonier. These distinguished officers never took to the water or to the field in 1757, but remained plastered one on either side of Pitt. This gave Pitt a chance which was denied to Mr. Asquith. I agree with General Ellison that, if war is to be conducted with the chance in our favour, we require a Minister—a Man—and not a War Council or a Sanhedrim. Further, I agree that that Minister requires to help him—to help him to arrive at decisions—a General Staff, representing the three arms of the Service, and, in future wars, the organised civilian population as well.

It is currently believed that we possess an Imperial General Staff. This belief is a very natural one, since there exists in much evidence a very distinguished officer whose official title is "Chief of the Imperial General Staff." He is, in point of fact, a Chief of a Staff which is non-existent, and his title is a ridiculous misnomer.

For some incomprehensible reason this word "Imperial" was introduced a few years back, before the words "General Staff." It cannot have been with the intention to mislead. But that has been the effect of an act which has been harmful to the organisation of our forces, as it has postponed for many years a real appreciation of where we stand.

There are signs in Parliament of a growing conviction that the solution of the problems posed by General Ellison in this very able book is to be found in a "Ministry of Defence." I doubt whether anyone who carefully reads this book will agree with this conclusion. The matter is not so simple as all that. At present the "Three Chiefs"—as they are called—of the three services, meet from time to time to exchange views and to discuss specific questions laid before them by the Secretariat of the Defence Committee. This is all to the good. But much more is required. A joint Staff College, where officers of the three arms can be instructed in high strategy and combined tactics under the same roof, where they can rub up against each other's prejudices, modify preconceived ideas, and look upon war as a disease that requires the combined treatment of surgery, medicine, and hygiene, is a primary and quite essential step to unity, first of Staff work on the highest plane, and, secondly, to Unity of Command. Meanwhile, I believe it to be essential that the meetings of the three chiefs should be presided over by a civilian Minister of high rank, whose word carries weight with his colleagues and with the Prime Minister.

It was all very well before the war to hold that the appointment of a Minister to such functions as these would derogate from the power of the Prime Minister. This belief, which I held myself, has been exploded by the greater dangers and necessities of war, of which General Ellison gives us more than a glimpse.

It would take too long to develop the thesis, but I am convinced that if we had possessed in 1914 a joint General Staff, presided over by such a Minister (let us say) as Lord Milner, the war would have been shortened by two years. A Ministry of Defence at the present time would be a clumsy expedient, and would mean the maximum of change with the minimum of efficiency. You cannot

sweep away three Secretaries of State, with their traditions, statu-
tory powers, and constitutional roots in our system of government,
by a stroke of the Parliamentary pen. Not Chatham or Lincoln,
perhaps not Napoleon, could administer three such services as ours,
and at the same time analyse our Imperial needs in the region of
defence, examine the proposals of experts who believe (as experts
should) in the invincibility each of his own special arm, and recon-
cile views that are bound to be divergent.

A Minister of Defence—yes. A Ministry of defence—no. The
machinery exists in embryo in the admirable Secretariat under Sir
Maurice Hankey, pending the growth of a Joint Imperial General
Staff. Some slight advance was made when the Prime Minister
appointed a Minister under himself as Chairman of the Defence
Committee. But the experiment was not seriously tried. Still, along
that road we are bound to travel, if, as General Ellison contends,
the financial necessities in time of peace, and the demands of strategy in time of war, are to be complied with in a manner consonant
with a form of government that rests on Parliamentary institutions,
which apparently are not yet on their last legs.

Sir Gerald Ellison is rendering a public service to his country-
men in drawing attention to this vital question in so telling a form.

# INTRODUCTION

*"The horrible tragedy of Gallipoli, where the best soldiers in the world were sacrificed to politicians' policies."*[2]

In these words the late Walter H. Page, the United States Ambassador to Great Britain in 1915, pronounces judgement on this disastrous campaign. They are the words of a man who possessed exceptional gifts of intuition, who knew better than most people what passed behind the scenes during the Great War, who had no axe of his own to grind and was singularly free from prejudice. Page was ever a staunch friend of England; he bore no ill-will to British politicians either individually or as a class. He was ever a seeker after truth, and once he was convinced of the truth he never hesitated to proclaim it forcibly and courageously. His judgement, therefore, cannot be set aside as negligible. Frankly, it is a terrible indictment.

Was Page right?

Where failure is at issue, a critic's denunciations demand exceptional scrutiny and examination. Success atones for a multitude of errors and the successful venture is apt not infrequently to be judged too leniently merely because it succeeded. Conversely, many a scheme, in itself perfectly sound and approved beforehand by the highest expert opinion, is subsequently condemned out of hand just because it failed in execution.

Accordingly, in appraising strategical values it is usually wise to eliminate as far as possible the factor of success or failure, into which an element of luck so largely enters, and concentrate rather on the underlying objects and potentialities of any particular project. Was the plan sound in itself? Had it the sanction of skilled expert opinion? Did the means available suffice to afford a reasonable prospect of success? Above all, would success at each stage in the development of the plan have led inevitably to the consummation of the ultimate objective, the enemy's complete defeat? In the answers to questions such as these lies the true criterion of strategical soundness or the reverse.

In making a study of the attack on the Dardanelles fortress in 1915 I have endeavoured to keep my mind free from bias due to

2      *The Life and Letters of Walter H. Page,* the United States Ambassador in Great Britain in 1915, vol. ii. p. 220.

the fact that the campaign ended in failure, and I ask my readers to adopt the same attitude. My primary object has been to elicit facts on which each one, for himself or herself, can form a judgement. My own conclusions, based on prolonged and anxious consideration of the known facts, and in no small measure as a result of personal observations during the campaign and of more recent reflections when I revisited the Gallipoli Peninsula, are clear to the point of conviction.

I hold it certain that the original conception of a naval attack against the fortress, as approved by the War Council on January 28, 1915, was unsound in the last degree. I assert that this plan never received the sanction of the responsible naval experts. I maintain that, later, the cooperation of the Army was obtained by methods of a very doubtful character. I personally am convinced that the land attack against the fortress never had a chance of success. Such assertions, made in the teeth of much that has been written and stated about this campaign, have to be justified. My belief is that they can be justified, and are in fact fully proven.

For the moment I deal with two issues only, both of first importance, namely, the unsoundness of the naval attack and the hopeless task the Army was set.

As regards the first of these issues, the events of 1922 speak for themselves. In that year a strong British squadron was supreme in the Sea of Marmora and covered Constantinople and the adjoining coast line with its guns; the town itself, the Ismid and Gallipoli Peninsulas, as well as Chanak and the hills surrounding it, were held by the land forces of the Allied Powers. (See maps.) Thus the situation at that time was far more favourable than could ever have been hoped for in 1915, had the fleet in March succeeded in forcing the Straits. Yet in 1922 Turkey was undismayed, and it is not reasonable to suppose that Enver and a Turkish army, much stronger and better equipped than that which Mustapha Kemal commanded, would have surrendered to a mere threat that Constantinople would be bombarded by the fleet's guns. In short, the fleet was powerless in the face of an unbeaten Turkish army, and for this reason the original conception of a naval attack against the Dardanelles fortress, apart from tactical difficulties, was thoroughly unsound strategically.

On the subject of the hopeless nature of the military attack against the fortress Lord Kitchener's appreciation, set out in full on p. 22, appears conclusive. The fortress, he reported officially in November, could not have been taken, even had a larger besieging army been employed than was actually available. What applied in November applied with equal, if not greater, force in April. No troops could have achieved what the Mediterranean Expeditionary Force was called on to accomplish.

Consider for a moment what the task was and how little was gained. The main Turkish position on the Kilid Bahr plateau and at Achi Baba is as formidable as can be found anywhere in the world. The attacking army never got within striking distance of this position; all it did was to gain minute strips of ground ashore, where for all practical purposes it was itself besieged during eight and a half months. (See maps)

During the whole campaign the Turks held up the attack on the outlying outpost positions of the fortress; they were throughout superior in point of numbers; they had been mobilised and had been training in their war formations for nearly nine months before the attack began; they knew every inch of a very difficult terrain; they were ably led; and they were close to Constantinople, their main base of supply. They were attacked at the very point where they were bound to be at their strongest.

On the other hand the Allies, owing to their other commitments, were from the start handicapped by want of trained men and by lack of ammunition and siege material; the naval attack had precluded surprise; and the difficulties of supply, especially when German submarines appeared on the scene, were beyond description or possibility of exaggeration.

And what a cost in lives, suffering, and treasure was paid for the meagre results obtained! No estimate has yet been made, or possibly could be made, of the drain on the material resources of the Empire that the attack on the Dardanelles fortress entailed. Enough to say that, in proportion to its size, this venture was probably the most expensive operation of war on which any nation has ever embarked. The complete lack of supplies or accommodation on the Peninsula itself; the necessity of bringing from Egypt drinking water for a large portion of the troops and animals; the length and insecurity of the communications; above all, the want of any well-found port nearer than Alexandria and the vast sums spent in consequence for demurrage on a great fleet of stationary store ships in Mudros roadstead: such considerations suffice in themselves to emphasise the costly character of this campaign.

The suffering, too, and the loss of health and vigour are also incalculable. At one time well over 1000 sick men a day were being evacuated from the Peninsula, suffering mostly from dysentery, which in August and September was epidemic. During these two months, it is officially recorded, 78 per cent, of the troops were suffering from dysentery and intestinal complaints, 64 per cent, had septic sores, and 50 per cent, of the troops who had been longest on the Peninsula showed symptoms of cardiac debility. In the end the whole expeditionary force was so worn out morally and physically that it was many months before some of the units could be regarded as again fit to take the field. In this respect Gallipoli outdoes the evil reputation of Walcheren.[3]

The numbers employed and the casualties have been stated officially. In April the gross strength of the Mediterranean Expeditionary Force is given as 124,000, rising gradually to 217,000 in August, and falling to 126,000 in December.[4] The total deaths from all causes are returned as 32,562; 7654 were missing or taken prisoners, and the total wound casualties were 78,261. (These are gross totals. The numbers in the fighting line were roughly 50 per cent, of the figures given above.) In addition, two French divisions were employed during most of the time, and their losses in proportion were not less than the British.

Truly the Gallipoli campaign was a horrible tragedy. But was so terrible a sacrifice the outcome of "politicians' policies"? For in that assertion lies the gravamen of Page's indictment. Whether it is a true charge or not those who read this volume must judge for themselves.

As I have indicated, I myself believe that the statement is in no sense an exaggeration. I hold firmly that neither the naval attack on the fortress nor the subsequent military campaign could, or would, ever have occurred had the naval and military experts been called

---

3      P.N. In 1809, during the Napoleonic Wars, Great Britain landed an expeditionary force of 39,000 men at Walcheren in the Netherlands, and suffered very high rates of dysentery, typhus, malaria, etc. They lost 4,000 men to disease, as against 109 men lost to the enemy.

4      These are gross totals. The numbers in the fighting line were roughly 50 percent of the figures given above.

on to consider the problem deliberately and in conjunction. In fact we know that, when a few years previously this very problem had been submitted to them to report on, their considered opinion had been so adverse that the government of the day had been forced to rule the operation of forcing the Straits altogether out of account.

In the following pages I have tried to make clear what the system of higher control was in 1915 which made it possible for expert opinion to be deliberately set aside, and the views of an amateur to be preferred to those of experienced seamen in a purely naval matter.

Were this all, this book would not have been written. Mere *post-mortem* bickerings and recriminations are seldom profitable and never edifying. But in this particular instance there is more than ordinary need for introspection and a close examination of facts and principles. Theoretically and in practice our system of conducting war, in so far as the higher control is concerned, remains today exactly what it was in 1914, and there is nothing whatever to prevent the astounding happenings of 1915 being repeated on some future occasion.

I go further and venture to predict that, unless and until the respective spheres of the politician and of the strategist are clearly defined apart from one another, disastrous consequences, if not inevitable, are at least probable. Whether the line of demarcation between politics and strategy which I have ventured to suggest in the concluding chapters is the best solution of a difficult problem I am not prepared to assert. What, however, I do maintain is that our whole system of the higher conduct of war needs fullest inquiry, and that such inquiry is a matter of consequence not to the Nation alone but for the Empire as a whole.

With the amazing example of Gallipoli before us, it seems intolerable that a science, whose mastery demands the devoted service and study of a lifetime, should remain for all time at the mercy of individual Ministers working in watertight compartments, or should continue a subject for casual discussion at assemblies of hard-worked politicians.

# CHAPTER I

## EXPERT PLANS

*"The root of Brevity and Brilliancy is Blunder."*

IN these words the late James Mason, one of the master minds in chess that England has produced, summarises the principles of the game. Restraint, patience, and persistency are the virtues he extols.

Have a plan, he says, almost any plan is better than none. Stick to your plan doggedly until it is clearly proved hopeless. Carry out your combination, bad though it be, and carefully consolidate your position. An attack, if checked, must be readily convertible into defence. Above all, as against a skilful opponent, beware of short cuts to victory. A mistimed attack is the height of indiscretion and all that this implies.

The analogy between chess strategy and war strategy, though not exact, cannot but strike the imagination. The principles underlying both are near akin. Both sciences are based on the example and precepts of great masters in the past; consequently, in both skill comes only as the result of much thought and prolonged study.

As between adversaries at all equally matched, the outcome in both is usually determined by the slow process of attrition. Accordingly in war, as in chess, patience and persistency are indispensable factors to success. In both an attempted short cut to victory, save as the inspiration of a master mind, leads almost inevitably to disaster.

In war, as in chess, a definite plan of action is essential, and during months, even years it may be, all other considerations must be subordinated to its due elaboration. Every detail must be attended to, every move of the adversary must be watched, and appropriate counter-measures must be taken. Nothing is more fatal than a constant change of plans.

The late war afforded two notable examples of strategical plans on the grand scale worked out in peace, and carried through to a logical conclusion when war supervened.

In 1905 Count Schlieffen, the Chief of the Great General Staff in Berlin, laid down the main lines of Germany's action in the event of a war on two fronts against France and Russia, acting conjointly. From that year onward this plan held good, and during the succeeding years it dominated German military policy. Regardless of expense, strategical railways were built, new army corps were added to the establishment, and secret measures were adopted for mobilising in an incredibly short space of time a vast number of reserve formations. As a result the world witnessed in August 1914 a sudden development of force such as had never previously been imagined. Even the French General Staff was taken by surprise. The immense scheme for the envelopment of the French field armies nearly succeeded. Its failure on the Marne only emphasised the inherent soundness of the strategical plan. Attack was readily converted into defence, and for nearly four years a defensive system, firmly established on French soil, remained unshaken.

The other outstanding example of strategical success based on a well-considered plan is afforded by our own Admiralty action prior to the war. On Trafalgar Day, 1904, Admiral Sir John Fisher became First Sea Lord, and he at once proceeded to give effect to the plan on which our whole naval policy was based from that time onwards. In Lord Fisher's own words: "There had been no such redistribution of strategical force since the days of Noah." All vessels that could neither fight nor run away were scrapped; outlying squadrons were reduced to a minimum; and by 1908 it could truthfully be said that 88 per cent of the British guns were trained on Germany.

The German high seas fleet and its harbours were now our primary objective. The abject surrender of the German Navy on November 20, 1918, was the crowning triumph of a policy ruthlessly and relentlessly pursued since 1904.

## THE FISHER-WILSON SCHEME

Two names will ever remain associated with the strategical conception which more than aught else contributed to the ultimate downfall of the Central Powers. During seven most critical years Admirals of the Fleet Lord Fisher and Sir Arthur Wilson, working in close conjunction, were the men who laid the foundations of victory. As the former has told us, they maintained the utmost secrecy regarding their plans, revealing them to no man.

In the early months of the Great War they once again collaborated in the direction of naval strategy. At the end of October 1914

Lord Fisher for a second time became First Sea Lord, and four days later he initiated a vast building programme "for a special purpose that had been decided on." This purpose, it is now known, was no less than the envelopment of Germany's north-western flank from the sea, and during the months that followed he urged forward with all his wonted forcefulness and energy the construction of a great Armada of monitors, river gunboats, submarine destroyers, motor barges (" beetles " they were christened later in Gallipoli), and small craft of all descriptions. All these were intended, as he himself states, "for great projects in the Baltic and North Sea."

"The programme of new vessels," he has told us in his *Memories*, "owed its inception to a great plan sketched out in secret memoranda, which it can confidently be asserted would have produced such great military results as would certainly have ended the war in 1915."

Fisher was no dreamer. Time and again he had been proved in practice to be right, after his plans had encountered most bitter opposition in many quarters, both naval and political. He himself had no doubts as to the ultimate success of the North Sea-Baltic scheme, and Wilson shared his views. Together these two men, one the great organiser, the other the consummate fleet leader, personified British naval tradition and doctrine.

**Their plan of 1914 was the logical development of the strategical conception that had held good since 1904.**

The fear the Germans had of a vigorous initiative on our part in the North Sea is, in itself, the most complete justification of the Fisher-Wilson strategy. Thus Admiral von Tirpitz writes as follows:

"The possibility that a battle might occur on the initiative of the enemy and not on ours constituted a danger for us. The English only needed to conduct a feint attack on our coast. An attack for example on Borkum or Sylt might easily force a battle on us. For such an attack they could bring up their whole fleet, including a number of their coastal vessels. The English did not even seek battle under these favourable circumstances."[5]

5          *My Memories*, by Grand Admiral von Tirpitz, vol. ii. p. 368. Compare with Tirpitz' views the following quotation from Corbett's *England in the Seven Years War* (vol. i. p. 270) with reference to a proposal by General Wolfe that five or six battalions should seize the Isle d' Aix, which commands the harbours of Rochefort and Rochelle. "The French, being the weaker afloat, had very properly taken the defensive with their

Undoubtedly some such plan as that indicated by Tirpitz was in Fisher's mind. For the production of the mechanical means to carry it out time was wanted, and time was all he asked for. This, however, was denied him.

"On May 14, 1915," he writes, "the War Council made it clear to me that the great projects in northern waters which I had in view in laying down the Armada of new vessels were at an end, and the further drain on our naval resources foreshadowed that evening convinced me that I could no longer countenance the Dardanelles operations, and the next day I resigned.

"It seemed to me that I was faced at last by a progressive frustration of my main scheme of naval strategy.

"Gradually the crowning work of war construction was being diverted and perverted from its original aim. The monitors, for instance, planned for the banks and shallows of northern waters, were sent off to the Mediterranean, where they had never been meant to operate."[6]

A somewhat remarkable feature of this change of plan deserves notice. Presumably Fisher's scheme had been examined and approved by the First Lord and the Government before the lavish expenditure of the nation's energies, that the construction of his Armada stood for, was sanctioned. Wonder, therefore, is increased that a plan, backed by the highest expert opinion and deliberately adopted, which already had cost many millions of pounds, should have been sacrificed and scrapped merely because a civilian Minister suddenly conceived a preference for another plan which he heralded as a short cut to victory.[7]

fleet, and ours unaided was powerless to break that defensive down. What Wolfe saw was that the Army could do what the Navy could not. By seizing an island vital to the French position they must either suffer the consequences, both during the war and at the balancing of accounts when it came to making peace, or else they must take the offensive with their fleet and expose it to destruction.

"The idea was absolutely sound. As a strategical device it is so obvious, so powerful, and so exactly suited to our peculiar resources, that the only wonder is it has been so seldom put in force. How many occasions could be counted when we have been baffled by our enemy assuming a naval defensive, and how seldom have we adopted clearly and resolutely this simple means of 'seeking out the enemy's fleet and destroying it!'"

6      *Memories*, by Lord Fisher, p. 73. (P.N. Lord Fisher wrote *Memories*, while Grand Admiral Von Tirpitz wrote *My Memories*.)

7      The expression "a short cut to victory" as applied to the naval

The broad question at issue is not so much whether this or that particular enterprise on the Belgian coast or at Sylt or Borkum or against the Kiel Canal was or was not feasible, as whether an active naval policy was to be pursued in the North Sea as opposed to one of mere passive expectancy. Further, it was a question of the concentration of our available naval forces in the main theatre instead of their being dissipated on a minor and, as it proved, a quite futile objective.

If our naval strategy in the latter half of 1915 had been of a more offensive character than it actually was, and if Fisher's Armada had been retained and maintained for its original purpose, instead of being diverted to the Aegean, the submarine peril, which threatened this country's existence in 1916-17, would, in all human probability, never have become acute.

Moreover, had the Fisher-Wilson plan been adhered to, the whole course of the war might well have been changed. Our position in the Baltic once assured, the advantages, not only naval and military, but also political and economic, would have been overwhelming. The blockade would have been complete, and the pressure on Germany would have been decisive.

Instead, the Baltic remained throughout the war a German lake, with results vividly depicted in the following letter, written by Lord Fisher in September 1917.

"Some headlines in the newspapers have utterly upset me! Terrible!
"'The German Fleet to assist land operations in the Baltic.'
"'Landing the German Army South of Reval.'

"We are five times stronger at sea than our enemies and here is a small fleet that we could gobble up in a few minutes playing the great vital Sea part of landing an army in the enemies' rear and probably capturing the Russian capital by Sea!"

"This is 'Holding the ring' with a vengeance!"

In forming a judgement on the naval attack against the Dardanelles, with all its consequences direct and indirect, the alternative plans it countered and supplanted—the Fisher-Wilson scheme and Lord Kitchener's Alexandretta project referred to in the next chapter—must never be lost to mind.

---

attack against the Dardanelles is Mr. Churchill's (vide *The World Crisis, 1915,* by the Rt. Hon. Winston Churchill, p. 49).

# ATTACK ON DARDANELLES FORTRESS
## Diary of Chief Events
### 1914
3rd Aug. Turkey mobilises her Army and Navy.

10th Aug. *Goeben* and *Breslau* enter the Marmora.

26th Sept. Dardanelles closed to traffic, and Russia's line of communication cut.

31st Oct. War with Turkey declared.

3rd Nov. British fleet bombards the Outer Forts of the Dardanelles fortress.

### 1915.
2nd Jan. Russia asks for a demonstration against Turkey.

28th Jan. War Council decides on a naval attack against the Dardanelles fortress.

16th Feby. Decision that Army must support the naval attack.

19th ,, Naval attack begins.

26th ,, Outer defences evacuated by the Turks.

17th Mar. General Hamilton arrives as Commander-in-Chief of Mediterranean Expeditionary Force.

18th ,, General attack by the Allied fleets fails.

19th ,, Lord Kitchener orders military action against the Peninsula.

25th April. Military landings on the Peninsula.

28th ,,Trench warfare begins.

10th May. Submarine menace. Supply and store ships ordered to Mudros.

17th ,, General Hamilton asks for two additional army corps.

7th June. Government decides to reinforce Mediterranean Expeditionary Force.

6th Aug. Battle of Sari Bair and landing at Suvla begin.

9th ,, Trench warfare again becomes general.

28th Oct. General Monro assumes command, and shortly after urges evacuation.

15th Nov. Lord Kitchener recommends evacuation.

27th ,, Blizzard causes 16,000 British casualties.

7th Dec. Government orders evacuation on Suvla and Anzac fronts.

20th ,, Evacuation of Suvla and Anzac completed.

28th ,, Government orders evacuation of Helles front.

### 1916.
8th Jany. Evacuation of the Gallipoli Peninsula completed.

# CHAPTER II

# TURKEY

CONCISELY stated, the political and military position at the beginning of 1915 was as follows: On the Western Front a position of deadlock had been reached, while in the East events were moving none too favourably for Russia, where lack of munitions was already beginning seriously to be felt. The position in the Balkans was critical in the extreme; Serbia was fighting gallantly against fearful odds; Greece and Rumania, though favourably inclined towards the Entente Powers, dared not move for fear of Germany; Bulgaria was frankly waiting on events and ready to side with whichever group of Powers could offer her the better terms. Italy still remained neutral.

## *THE TURKISH ARMY*

At the end of October 1914 the Balkan situation had been further complicated owing to Turkey having been dragged into the war by Germany and her henchmen, Enver and Talaat. She had already mobilised her Army and her Navy on August 3.

**Consequently in January 1915 she had already had five months in which to consolidate her position and train her Army in its war formations.**

In this respect the situation was very different from what it had been in 1911, when Turkey was caught unprepared by Bulgaria and suffered disastrous defeats in less than a fortnight after war was declared.[8] The mobilisation in 1914, worked out previously in all its details with true German thoroughness, proved most successful. The standing army on a war footing was approximately 600,000 strong, and there was about the same number of men Hable to be called up, and available to build up reserve formations and make good the wastage of war.

Roughly speaking, 200,000 regulars faced the Russians in the Caucasus, 100,000 were in Syria and Palestine, and another 100,000 garrisoned Mesopotamia and Southern Arabia and var-

8    P.N. The two Balkan Wars took place in 1912 and 1913, when Bulgaria, Serbia, Montenegro, and Greece formed the Balkan League and attacked the Ottomans.

ious coast defences and fortresses. The flower of the Army, some 200,000 strong, was kept in and near Constantinople to serve as the mainstay of the Government, and to act as a central reserve for reinforcing threatened points.

Enver Pasha, now thirty-two years of age, was virtually a dictator. Appointed Vice Generalissimo of the Ottoman naval and military forces in August 1914, his position was unassailable so long as the Constantinople Army remained undefeated. Here, as ever in continental warfare, the defeat of the main Turkish Army was the one thing that mattered—a point the soldier readily appreciates but one which too often escapes the lay mind.

**This elementary principle of strategy would appear to have been altogether lost sight of, when the idea of a purely naval attack against the Dardanelles was conceived.**

## THE DARDANELLES FORTRESS

For many years the Turkish Army had been organised and trained under German supervision, and during 1914 Germany's efforts to increase its efficiency were redoubled. In December 1913 Marshal Liman von Saunders, with seventy selected officers, reached Constantinople, and from the following August onwards naval and military officers, as well as mechanics and artisans, continued to pour into the Turkish capital from Germany. Before the end of the war there are said to have been no less than 800 German officers in the Turkish service.

The most notable of the new arrivals was Admiral von Usedom who, in September 1914, became responsible for the efficiency of the Bosphorus and Dardanelles defences. What he and his expert subordinates, working in close conjunction with the German military mission, were able to achieve is a long and interesting story in itself. For the moment all that need be said is that

**by February 1915 the Dardanelles fortress, on both its sea and land fronts, had become as formidable a system of defence as existed anywhere in the world.**[9]

9          The military student would be well advised to look up the British Official History of the Siege of Port Arthur in 1904. A comparison of the methods adopted by the Japanese on that occasion with our own in 1915 is of great interest. Achi Baba is a replica of 203 Metre Hill, which proved to be the key of the Russian fortress. Its capture entailed prodigious efforts and huge losses for the Japanese, who had with them

An impression exists that the defences of the fortress were taken seriously in hand only when the Allied naval attack threatened in February, and that till then the work done had been negli-gible. Such a view, however, is wholly erroneous. During the winter months German brains and numerous Turkish labour battalions had been busy, and nothing that human ingenuity could devise had been left undone to render the fortress impregnable.

Sir Ian Hamilton has told us that, when in March he reconnoi-tred the Peninsula from the sea, his staff estimated that the recent work on the Bulair Lines alone must have occupied 10,000 men for at least a month. But such work had not been confined to Bulair. Its defences were but a sample of the digging and entangling that in previous months had been carried out on the main Kilid Bahr-Achi Baba line of defence in Europe and on the extensive Troy position in Asia, as well as on the outpost defences of the fortress.

Lord Kitchener's own appreciation, quoted later in this chapter, of the immense strength of the Kilid Bahr-Achi Baba position is in no sense an exaggeration. In May, too, General Birdwood, writing to Lord Kitchener, compared Kilid Bahr to the Rock of Gibraltar. The comparison is not inapt. Nothing more formidable can well be imagined.

"Achi Baba is really a fortress."[10]

## THE DARDANELLES GARRISON

Nor in February or even earlier is it likely that the defenders of the fortress would have been found less watchful or less numer-ous than they proved to be when our Expeditionary Force landed in April. It is true that a legend exists, and receives credence, of a small party of British Marines, at some time early in 1915, stroll-ing unconcernedly to the top of Achi Baba. The story, however, is purely mythical.

The facts are these. On November 3, 1914, the Outer Defences of the fortress were bombarded by orders from the Admiralty, the magazine of Sedd el Bahr fort exploded, and a considerable portion of its garrison was killed or wounded. After that date no British

---

a powerful siege train. The strength of the besiegers was consistently maintained at 100,000 men; before the end of the siege the Port Arthur garrison was less than 20,000 strong.

10        Telegram from General Hamilton to Lord Kitchener. May 10th.

sailor, soldier, or marine landed on the Peninsula save as an act of war.

On February 26, 1915, after further bombardments by the fleet, the Turks deliberately evacuated the Outer Defences, and shortly afterwards small naval parties, under cover of heavy fire from the guns of the fleet, entered two forts which lie within a stone's-throw of the water's edge and demolished guns in them, But the moment they attempted to go beyond the narrow limits of the forts and the clusters of houses adjoining them, they were held up by the fire of Turkish infantry, which naval gunnery was impotent to overcome. Already at this early stage the inability of the flat-trajectory ship's gun to deal with concealed artillery and trenches was pronounced.

So much for the legendary slackness of the garrison.

Touching its alleged weakness, statements are more precise. Thus Mr. Churchill writes: "Three divisions in February could have occupied the Gallipoli Peninsula with little fighting. Five could have captured it after March 18. Seven were insufficient at the end of April, but nine might just have done it. Eleven might have sufficed at the beginning of July. Fourteen were to prove insufficient on August 7."[11]

Statements such as these deserve careful examination in the light of ascertained facts.

From the outbreak of war in October till the middle of February there were available on the spot for the defence of the fortress, over and above the fixed garrisons of the forts and coast defences, two regular divisions, each 12,000 to 13,000 strong. One division was on the Gallipoli Peninsula, the other on the Asiatic side of the Dardanelles. So long as no land attack threatened this mobile garrison was deemed sufficient.

Later events, however, proved clearly enough that the Turkish High Command and its German advisers were not going to leave 150,000 men idle round Constantinople, if and when hostile land forces showed signs of battering at the Sultan's front door. Equally they were not guilty of the military crime of dissipating their reserves before the direction and the strength of the real attack were apparent. But the moment the slightest indication of such an attack became evident they moved, and moved effectively.

---

11      *The World Crisis*, 1915, p. 394.

The appearance in the Aegean in February of only two *battalions* of marines sufficed to draw two *divisions* from Constantinople to the Peninsula. The arrival of an Australian brigade at Mudros early in March at once brought down another division from the central reserve. Later, division followed division in exact proportion as our attack was reinforced. Throughout the campaign the defence kept the upper hand in point of numbers.

**Any attack, other than a surprise attack, launched by the Allies from November onwards, would certainly have been met with superior numbers on the part of the defence.**

Surprise on land was, of course, precluded by the preliminary naval action and by the publicity given to our aims in London.

Mr. Churchill's notion of the weakness of the garrison in February is doubtless due to the mistake the amateur so often makes of assuming that, because a vital point is apparently not held in strength at a particular moment, it can therefore be easily captured. When, however, as happened in this instance, reserves are available and within easy reach, the experienced soldier is very chary of accepting any such assumption.

If in 1915 Mr. Churchill's expressed views were shared by the other members of the Council in London who controlled the Gallipoli campaign, much that now seems incomprehensible can be readily explained.

## *LORD KITCHENER'S VIEW*

Lord Kitchener's appreciation, not only of the strength of the fortress, but also of the chances of its capture, is one which history will certainly endorse. No one had opposed abandoning the Gallipoli enterprise more strongly than he. On November 3, 1915, he telegraphed from London to General Birdwood:

"I absolutely refuse to sign orders for evacuation."

Twelve days later, after he had visited the Peninsula and had consulted the men on the spot, his report to the Prime Minister urging evacuation was as follows:

**To gain what we hold has been a most remarkable feat of arms. The country is much more difficult than I imagined, and the Turkish positions at Achi Baba and Kilid Bahr are natural**

fortresses of the most formidable nature, which, if not taken
by surprise at first, could be held against very serious attack by
larger forces than have been engaged, even if those forces had
proper lines of communication to support them. This latter want
is the main difficulty in carrying out successful operations on the
Peninsula. . . . Everyone has done wonders, both on sea and land,
when the natural difficulties that have had to be surmounted are
considered.[12]

If anyone inclines to doubt the truth of this appreciation, let him
go to the Peninsula and judge for himself.

The conclusion is inevitable.

The Navy's previous action had precluded surprise.

For want of a harbour to serve as a land base, greater numbers
than were actually landed could not have been supplied and adequately maintained ashore. Above all, no means existed for landing
and bringing into action the mass of heavy siege guns, ammunition,
and stores requisite for so tremendous an operation as the reduction of a first-class fortress.

**To besiege or assault the Dardanelles fortress was, therefore,
not a feasible operation of war. This view had, for years, been held
consistently by the General Staff.**

## THE ALLIES' RESOURCES

Clearly, when Turkey entered the war, the Entente Powers could
not afford to neglect her challenge. A Holy War[13] had been pro-
claimed, and in every bazaar throughout the East and in Northern
Africa the Khalif's action excited keen interest. Turkey neglected,
or worse still Turkey victorious, menaced the interests of every
European Power from the Straits of Gibraltar to the easternmost
boundaries of the British Raj.

Above all, by closing in September 1914 the narrow waterway
between the Mediterranean and the Black Sea, Turkey had not
only cut Russia's main line of communication, but had also denied
the rich cornfields of Southern Russia and Rumania, and the oil-

---

12      *Report of the Dardanelles Commission*, Part II. para. 126.
13      P.N. Germany encouraged the Ottoman Sultan to declare Jihad
when World War One began, to energize his soldiers and sow unrest in
Allied territories where Muslims lived.

fields of the Caucasus, to the opponents of the Central Powers. Russia's currency was collapsing in consequence; and many thousands of tons of much-needed British shipping were locked up in the Black Sea ports.

Prompt measures were taken to meet the challenge. British and French warships blockaded the Turkish coast line from the Persian Gulf to the head of the Aegean Sea. Russian Army corps attacked in the Caucasus, and before the end of November an Indian division was landed not far from Basra in Mesopotamia.

In Egypt four divisions, one from India, one of Territorials, and two from Australia and New Zealand, together with a large body of mounted troops, were concentrated by the end of the year. Of these divisions three were only partially trained; in fact, the serious training of the Australian and New Zealand troops in their war formations had only just begun when the New Year opened. They were in no sense ready for mobile operations on a large scale.

In Tunis, France was assembling a division, composed mainly of colonial and native troops, to be held in readiness for all eventualities.

## THE ALEXANDRETTA PROJECT

In January 1915 Lord Kitchener was engaged in maturing his plans for checkmating any attempt by the enemy to stir up trouble in the East. With unerring insight he had recognised where, with the least effort and the greatest effect, a deadly blow could be struck.

A force landed in the Gulf of Alexandretta and thrown across the Baghdad railway, which skirts the Gulf, would at one stroke have severed Turkey's main line of communication eastwards.

**The Ottoman Empire would have been literally cut in two.**

Owing to the railway tunnels through the mountain ranges east and west of the Gulf being still unfinished in 1915, any effective reply to this master-stroke was practically precluded. Turkish armies advancing, either from the west or from the east, to attack a hostile army entrenched across the railway would, from their railheads beyond the mountain ranges, have had some 80 miles of mountain tracks and difficult roads to traverse, and without abundant mechanical transport—and this Turkey did not possess—the supply problem would have been well-nigh insoluble. Moreover, the local population, largely Armenian, would certainly have aided and abetted the invaders.

The conditions, in fact, were ideally perfect for the sort of stroke which, as so often has happened in our history, Sea Power enables us to deliver with deadly effect. Had the Alexandretta scheme been adhered to and carried through with the whole might of India, Australia, and New Zealand behind it, together with moderate assistance from home, Turkish resistance would almost certainly have collapsed before the end of 1915.

There would have been no Mesopotamian campaign, no Armenian massacres, no toiling through the sands of the Sinai Peninsula, no Gaza battles and no fighting in Palestine. In all human probability Bulgaria would never have joined the Central Powers, Serbia would have been saved, and the Russian debacle might never have occurred. Lastly, we would have been spared the naval humiliation of the Dardanelles defeat and the vast sacrifice of human life and national treasure that the Gallipoli venture entailed.

**Taken in conjunction with Lord Fisher's strategical plan, with which it in no way collided, a determined attack on the Baghdad railway, from the Gulf of Alexandretta, would almost certainly have shortened the war by years.**

What the opportunity amounted to is made clear by the following extracts from Field Marshal von Hindenburg's reminiscences of the war.

"Perhaps not the whole course of the war," he writes,"but certainly the fate of our Ottoman Ally could have been settled out of hand, if England had secured a decision in that region, or even seriously attempted it. Possession of the country south of the Taurus would have been lost to Turkey at a blow if the English had succeeded in landing in the Gulf of Alexandretta.

"In so doing they would have severed the main artery of Trans-Taurian Turkey, through which fresh blood and other revitalising forces flowed to the Syrian, Mesopotamian and a part of the Caucasian armies.

"The protection of the Gulf of Alexandretta was entrusted to a Turkish army which contained scarcely a single unit fit to fight; every man who could be of use in the fighting line was gradually transferred to Syria or Mesopotamia. Moreover, coast protection by artillery at this point was more a figment of the Oriental imagination than a military reality.

"Enver Pasha exactly described the situation to me in the words: 'My only hope is that the enemy has not discovered our weakness at this critical spot.' It seemed impossible that the English High Command should not know the true state of the coast defences in this theatre.

"If ever there was a prospect of a brilliant strategic feat it was here. Such a campaign would have made an enormous impression on the whole world, and unquestionably would have had a far-reaching effect on our Turkish Ally.

"Why did England never make use of her opportunity here?"[14]

The answer is tragically simple. General Birdwood's army corps in Egypt was, in February 1915, to have undertaken this very operation, and the necessary orders for action after landing had actually been issued and explained to all concerned. But on February 16, as we shall learn later, a decision was come to in London which diverted all available troops in Egypt for the purpose of supporting the naval attack against the Dardanelles fortress.

**Lord Kitchener's strategical plan suffered the same fate as Lord Fisher's, and for the same reason.**

Later, when it had been decided to abandon the Gallipoli enterprise, Lord Kitchener reverted to the Alexandretta project and strongly recommended its being undertaken. But by then the naval and military staffs of both France and Great Britain, as well as the statesmen of both countries, were satiated with amphibious warfare and no scheme of that nature, however enticing, would tempt them a second time after the Aegean experience. Moreover, at the end of 1915 we were already committed to the Salonika venture.[15]

## A NAVAL DEMONSTRATION

On January 2, 1915, a message to Lord Kitchener was received from the Commander-in-Chief of the Russian Army expressing a

---

14    *Out of My Life*, by Marshal von Hindenburg, p. 294.
15    P.N. Britain and France both committed troops to Salonika to counter Bulgaria's offensive against Serbia, and to keep Greece neutral, further diluting the forces that could be committed to Gallipoli and the Straits.

hope that a demonstration might be made against Turkey, in order to relieve the pressure being felt at the moment by the Russians in the Caucasus. Such a request from an Ally who had made, and was making, very great sacrifices in the common cause appealed forcibly to the Secretary of State for War, who pressed for a naval demonstration against the Dardanelles as the only practical step. In making this suggestion to the First Lord of the Admiralty he stated: "We have no troops to land anywhere. . . . We shall not be ready for anything big for some months."

Without denuding the Western Front of British and Indian troops, it is certain that, in January 1915, no force was forthcoming capable of meeting the Constantinople army on its own ground with any chance of success.

A naval demonstration in itself would, however, have proved advantageous for two reasons. First, as events proved, it would have afforded the Russians the relief they sought. The destruction by naval gunfire of the Outer Forts of the Dardanelles fortress—a feasible and safe operation—in conjunction with the concentration in the Aegean Islands of small bodies of troops would have kept the Turkish High Command on tenterhooks for weeks and possibly for months. We have already seen that the arrival in February of quite insignificant detachment of British troops in the neighbourhood of the fortress caused its garrison to be at once heavily reinforced, and incidentally eased the pressure on the Russians in the Caucasus.

Secondly, a demonstration, such as Lord Kitchener asked for, would, if cleverly worked, have materially assisted the execution of the Alexandretta project. It was in fact a most useful, if not indispensable, complement to the strategical plan he had in mind at the time.

It only remains to add that, within a week of the Grand Duke's appeal being received in London, the urgent need for affording assistance to the Russian Army in the Caucasus had disappeared. That appeal had arisen out of anxiety regarding a big Turkish movement, which in December had been developing on a wide front against the Russian communications on the Kars-Erzeroum road. But on January 4 this movement ended most disastrously for the Turks at Sarikamisch, and after that date the Russians were more than able to hold their own in the Caucasus.

Accordingly, our strategy at the beginning of 1915 was not hampered, as is sometimes alleged, owing to the supposed desperate straits of our Ally.

Precipitate action at the Dardanelles, or elsewhere, was not required. Moreover, persistence in the attempt to reach Constantinople, after the need for the desired demonstration had passed, had the effect of creating grave doubts in the Russian mind as to our ultimate intentions.

## THE CHANGE OF PLAN

In any approach to the subject of the naval attack against the Dardanelles defences and its sequel, the military landing on the Gallipoli Peninsula, one fact must be kept clearly before the mind. Two plans already existed. Both were the conception of practical men; both were, or would shortly have been, within the compass of the forces and means available; both, in the event of success, promised decisive results; both met with a similar fate.

**The Dardanelles attack stood for an abrupt and all-embracing change of strategical conception. With the effective conduct of operations in the hands of Fisher and Kitchener, such a change of plan could not have occurred. The Gallipoli landing would never have taken place.**

# CHAPTER III

# THE VALOUR OF IGNORANCE

THE narrative of the events which led to a naval attack, in con-tradistinction to a naval demonstration, being undertaken against the Dardanelles fortress is fully set forth in the first report of the Special Commission, presided over first by Lord Cromer and after his death by Sir William Pickford, which in 1916-17 inquired "into the origin, inception, and conduct of the operations of war in the Dardanelles and Gallipoli." This report is one of the most important State documents ever published, laying bare as it does in plainest fashion the nature of our machinery for the higher conduct of war as it existed in 1914-15. It was issued in 1917 at a critical period of the war, and consequently has never received the amount of attention it deserves.

Unfortunately, too, neither the sworn evidence of all the chief actors in this great drama—statesmen, sailors, soldiers, and civilians alike—nor certain important documents on which the reports are based have ever been published in full, and a most dangerous prec-edent has been thereby established.

**This is the first occasion in this country on which evidence given before a War Commission has been withheld from the public.**

Without a careful and prolonged study of the two reports issued by the Dardanelles Commission, no adequate idea of the events with which they deal is possible. Here all that can be attempted is to state briefly the leading facts of a very remarkable story, as well as opinions relevant to the facts expressed by the Commission in its reports.[16]

The War Council, it should be explained, consisted in January 1915 of seven Cabinet Ministers, including Mr. Asquith the' Prime Minister, Lord Kitchener the Secretary of State for War, Mr. Chur-

---

16     The reports were issued by the Stationery Office, Imperial House, Kingsway, W.C.2. Part I. at 6d., Part II. at 2s.
References to the text of the reports given as footnotes in this and the following chapters, are marked D.C. The number I, or II. indicates the first or the second report as the case may be, and the final number the paragraph (unless page is stated) to which reference is made.

chill the First Lord of the Admiralty, and Sir Edward Grey, the Foreign Minister.[17]

Mr. Balfour who was not a member of the Government, Lord Fisher the First Sea Lord, Admiral of the Fleet Sir Arthur Wilson, and Lieutenant-General Sir James Wolfe Murray the Chief of the Imperial General Staff, regularly attended the meetings.

It must be added, too, that since the escape of the *Goeben* and the *Breslau* into the Sea of Marmora in August 1914, a strong naval squadron, under Vice-Admiral Carden, had been blockading the entrance to the Dardanelles.

On January 2, when Lord Kitchener suggested a naval demonstration, "the First Lord thought it was possible to convert and extend that demonstration into an attempt to force a passage. . . . The views entertained by Mr. Churchill at the time as to the prospect of success of a purely naval operation were somewhat more optimistic than was warranted by the opinion of the experts. Under these circumstances, Lord Kitchener grasped, perhaps rather too eagerly, at the proposal to act through the agency of the fleet alone."[18]

As regards naval action, Lord Kitchener was as much a layman as any of the civilian members of the Council. He himself made this clear in a statement he read out at a Council meeting on May 14. "When," he said," the Admiralty proposed to force the passage of the Dardanelles by means of the fleet alone, I doubted whether the attempt would succeed, but was led to believe it possible by the First Lord's statements of the power of the *Queen Elizabeth* and the Admiralty Staff paper showing how the operation was to be conducted. ... I regret I was led to agree in the enterprise by the statements made, particularly as to the power of the *Queen Elizabeth*, of which I had no means of judging."

## MEETING OF JANUARY 13

At a meeting on January 13, Mr. Churchill said he had interchanged telegrams with Admiral Carden in regard to the possibilities of a naval attack on the Dardanelles. His reply was that it might be possible to demolish the forts one by one and to this end he had submitted a plan. Lord Kitchener thought the plan was

17    D.C. I. page 47.
18    D.C. I. 53.

worth trying. We could leave off the bombardment if it did not prove effective.[19]

After hearing the views expressed by Lord Kitchener and Mr. Churchill—Lord Fisher, Sir Arthur Wilson, and Sir James Wolfe Murray remaining silent—the War Council decided that **the Admiralty should prepare for a naval expedition in February to bombard and take the Gallipoli Peninsula, with Constantinople as its objective.**[20]

The remarkable wording of this very remarkable decision suffices to show how the case for an attack had been presented to the Council. The hand that wrote it was presumably the hand of the Prime Minister, the voice that instigated it was certainly the voice of the First Lord.

Mr. Churchill without doubt meant that the force to be employed was to be purely naval. On this point all the witnesses examined by the Commission were unanimous.[21]

One of the main reasons advanced in the first instance which appealed to Lord Kitchener and everybody was that, if it was a purely naval business, it could be abandoned at any time without loss of prestige.

Recent evidence published by Lord Grey of Falloden strongly endorses this view.

"The attack on the Dardanelles," he writes, "was agreed to on the express condition that it should be a naval operation only; it was under no circumstances to involve the use of troops. ... If it did not succeed, it was to be treated as a demonstration and abandoned.

**"It was on this condition only that Kitchener agreed to it."**[22]

---

19      D.C. I. 66 and 67.
20      D.C. I. 69.
21      D.c. I. 71.
22      *Twenty-five Years*, 1892-1916, by Viscount Grey of Falloden, K.G., vol. II, p. 76.

## THE EXPERT VIEW

The Dardanelles Commission in its report deals at some length with the views of the three most eminent experts at the Admiralty at the time when the naval attack was under discussion, viz. Admirals of the Fleet Lord Fisher and Sir Arthur Wilson, and Admiral Sir Henry Jackson.

The last-named officer was specially charged with the study of the Eastern theatre of war, and on January 5 he wrote a note on forcing the passage of the Dardanelles and threatening Constantinople "without military co-operation."[23] In it he dwelt on the minimum force required to undertake the operation, on the losses which would probably be involved in any attempt "to reach the Straits," to which he was strongly opposed, and on the necessity of providing a large supply of ammunition. He pointed out clearly the many technical difficulties of the undertaking and emphasised the unenviable position the fleet would be in, even if it reached Constantinople, "unless there were a large military force to occupy the town." The bombardment of the town alone "would not," he maintained, "greatly affect the distant military operations."

In his evidence before the Commission in 1916 Admiral Jackson stated that he did not consider that an attempt by the fleet alone to pass the Dardanelles was a "feasible operation." He thought that Mr. Churchill had been "very much more sanguine" than he and other experts were. He did not consider it part of his duty to interfere unduly with naval policy unless he was invited to do so by some superior. He had no responsibilities except just for the staff work he did.[24]

Sir Arthur Wilson stated in his evidence that he was "moderately adverse" to the plan of bombarding the Dardanelles, as he thought other things might be better.[25] In other words he preferred the North Sea-Baltic plan. Mr. Churchill admitted that if Admiral Wilson had been asked at a Council Meeting to give a vote on the naval attack he would have voted in the negative.

## LORD FISHER'S ATTITUDE

Lord Fisher's attitude, inasmuch as he was the First Lord's offi-

23   D.C. I. 57.
24   D.C. I. 60.
25   D.C. I. 88.

cial adviser on operations, needs fuller investigation. As we know, he had his own strategical plan of which he expected great things, and he was not likely to approve of a change of plan, unless he was fully persuaded that the change was for the better. It is clear, however, that he was not so obsessed with one idea that he could see no advantages in any other strategical conception. In fact, early in January he was urging amphibious operations on a vast scale against Turkey. His suggestion was that 75,000 seasoned troops should be brought from the Western Front and landed at Besika Bay, that Alexandretta should be occupied, and Haifa threatened. A Greek army was to go for Gallipoli, and the Bulgarians for Constantinople, and to crown all a British squadron was to force the Dardanelles.[26]

This plan is mainly of interest as showing that **Lord Fisher recognised from the start that the defeat of Turkey was primarily a military and not a naval matter.**

"The Army ought to have done it all along" was his remark, so Mr. Churchill tells us, when, after the naval failure on March 18, the renewal of the naval attack was abandoned and the Army was called on to operate.[27]

A naval and military operation on a sufficient scale would certainly have met with Lord Fisher's approval, but his face was set resolutely against naval action alone where coast fortifications were concerned. In 1906, when First Sea Lord, he had signed a memorandum in which action by the Navy alone against the Dardanelles was strongly deprecated; moreover, he was never tired of quoting Nelson's dictum that the sailor who attacks a fort is a fool.

When writing to Mr. Churchill in May, after he had resigned his appointment as First Sea Lord, Lord Fisher fully explained his attitude in regard to the naval attack. "I could give you no better proof," he wrote, "of my desire to stand by you than my having remained by you in this Dardanelles business up to the last moment against the strongest conviction of my life as stated in the Dardanelles Defence Committee Memorandum."[28]

Holding such views, Lord Fisher was not the man to keep them to himself. The charwomen at the Admiralty, he says, must have

26      *World Crisis*, 1915, p. 95.
27      *World Crisis*, 1915, p. 234.
28      Idem, p. 362.

known them. Certainly the First Lord did.

## LORD FISHER'S MEMORANDUM

On January 25 Lord Fisher sent the First Lord a long memorandum on Naval Policy.[29] He advocated patience and a policy of
steady pressure on Germany. "The sole justification," he said, "of
coastal bombardments and attacks by the Fleet on fortified places,
such as the contemplated prolonged bombardment of the Dardanelles forts by our Fleet, is to force a decision at sea, and so far and
no farther can they be justified.... Even the older ships should not
be risked, for they cannot be lost without losing men and they form
our only reserve behind the Grand Fleet." Lord Fisher insisted
from the first that a loss of twelve battleships had to be faced, if an
attack against the Straits was pushed home.

The following note accompanied the memorandum:

"FIRST LORD,—I have no desire to continue a useless resistance in the War Council to plans I cannot concur in, but I would
ask that the enclosed may be printed and circulated to its members
before the next meeting.—F."

This request was not complied with. The memorandum, with
a reply to it by the First Lord, dated January 27, was sent to the
Prime Minister alone. The members of the Council were left in
ignorance of Lord Fisher's views.

## SILENCE OF THE EXPERTS

**Briefly stated, the reason which induced not only Lord Fisher
but also Sir Arthur Wilson and Sir James Wolfe Murray to
remain silent at the Council meetings was the view they all
held that they were in no sense members of the Council. They
regarded themselves merely as experts in attendance with their
Minister at a meeting of a Cabinet Committee.[30]**

They were not there to speak unless their opinion was asked for,
and it seldom was. " Mr. Churchill," said Lord Fisher, "was my
Chief, and it was silence or resignation. I did not want to have an
altercation with my Chief at the Council."[31]

---

29    *World Crisis*, 1915, p. 154.
30    D.C. I. 18 and 19
31    D.C. I. 87.

This view of the experts as to their position is discussed more fully in Chapters VI and VII.

On the other hand, "the Chairman and Ministerial members looked to the naval and military experts to express their opinions if they dissented from the views put forward by the heads of their respective departments."

"As the experts did not express their opinions the Council was in technical matters guided wholly by the views laid before them by the Secretary of State for War and by the First Lord of the Admiralty."[32]

## ADMIRALTY PROCEDURE

Thus it came about that the First Lord, a civilian and an amateur, became the sole exponent of naval policy before the body in which the direction of the war was vested. Such a position could be justified only on two assumptions: first, that he spoke with the authority of the Board of Admiralty behind him, and, secondly, that he explained to the War Council fully and fearlessly the arguments against, as well as for, any particular plan of strategy brought to its notice. That neither of these conditions was fulfilled is made evident by the findings of the Dardanelles Commission.

This matter is of such vast national importance that their findings have to be quoted in full.

"It is abundantly clear," so runs the report, "that, although no formal or official change was made, the spirit in which the business of the Admiralty was conducted underwent a great transformation immediately after the outbreak of the war. The Board of Admiralty sank into insignificance, its place being taken by the War Staff Group.[33]

"The Board was, even to a less extent than previously, able to assume any 'collective responsibility' for the general conduct of affairs. The individual numbers of the Board were not kept well-informed of passing events. They were not consulted before the naval attack on the Dardanelles was made. It is clear that Mr. Asquith was ill-informed as regards the methods under which Admiralty

---

32      D.C. 1. 29.
33      The War Staff Group after November 1914 consisted of Mr. Churchill, Lord Fisher, Sir Arthur Wilson, and Admiral Oliver (the Chief of the Staff), with two Secretaries.

business was conducted when he stated to the Commission that the members of the War Council 'were entitled to assume' that any views laid before them by the First Lord of the Admiralty 'was the considered opinion of the Board of Admiralty as a whole.'"[34]

**In plain English, so far as the conduct of war operations was concerned, the Board of Admiralty disappeared for the time being, and the body which for 300 years the nation had regarded as the sure custodian of its naval interests ceased to exist.**

Furthermore, every constitutional safeguard fell into disuse. Even the time-honoured custom of Admiralty orders being issued by the Secretary in the name of "My Lords" no longer obtained.

## METHODS OF CORRESPONDENCE

Instead, the First Lord habitually corresponded directly, in the first person, with the Admirals in command of fleets regarding their operations and their appointments. How such a practice came into being and how far it had Government sanction is not clear. The Admiralty does not readily render up its secrets, and it is from the report of the Dardanelles Commission and from Mr. Churchill's and Lord Fisher's own writings that the methods in force at the time have to be reconstructed.

That the practice existed there is no room for doubt. Take for example the all-important telegram which proved to be the source and origin of the naval attack against the Dardanelles and of the ill-fated military enterprise against the Gallipoli Peninsula. It is worded as follows:

*Admiralty to Vice-Admiral Carden*

*January 3, 1915.*

From the First Lord:

"Do you consider the forcing of the Dardanelles by ships alone a practicable operation?

"It is assumed older battleships fitted with mine-bumpers would be used, preceded by colliers and other merchant craft as mine bumpers and sweepers.

"Importance of results would justify severe loss.

---

34    D.C. I. 37

"Let me know your views."[35]

A volume might be written on the psychological effect of such a message on its recipient.[36] It is the sort of missive Napoleon used to address to his Admirals. In sea matters Napoleon ever remained an amateur, and if an Admiral received such a letter he knew well that he had better reciprocate his master's views. If he failed readily to respond, he did so at his peril. The Emperor always had someone ready and available to take his place.

Take again the further telegram of January 6 in reply to Admiral Carden, who on the 5th had stated that he considered the Dardanelles "might be forced by extended operations with large number of ships."

It runs as follows:

### First Lord to Admiral Carden

"High authorities here concur in your opinion. Forward detailed particulars showing what force would be required for extended operations. How do you think it should be employed, and what results could be gained?"[37]

As regards this telegram it is to be observed that Mr. Churchill admitted to the Commission that "when he spoke of 'high authorities' he meant only Sir Henry Jackson and Admiral Oliver (the Chief of the Staff), both of whom had expressed their opinion to him verbally."[38]

---

35        *World Crisis*, 1915, p. 97.
36        Admiral de Robeck's evidence before the Dardanelles Commission should be read in this connection. (See D.C. I. no.) "We were told," he said, "to bombard these forts, so we did it."
Q. You were told from the Admiralty? A. Yes.
Q. Was that your view of what Admiral Carden thought— that he was told to do it—that he had no discretion?
A. I think he was directly told to get on and do it.
[Admiral de Robeck succeeded Admiral Carden, who was invalided on March 16, in command of the Dardanelles fleet.]
37        D.C. I. 56.
38        Lord Barham, when First Lord, would not issue an order, however urgent, without getting it countersigned by two other members of the Board, and then it was issued by the Secretary in the name of the Lords Commissioners.
We have travelled far since 1805. Neither of the officers who gave their verbal assent to this telegram of January 6 was a member of the Admiralty Board.

"Vice-Admiral Carden," so runs the report, "would naturally suppose that Lord Fisher was included among those who concurred in this view."

In this connection a passage in Lord Fisher's *"Memories"* (p. 111) is so apposite that its reproduction seems justified. "A Chief of the Staff," he writes, "was planked into the Admiralty and indirectly supplanted the First Sea Lord. I won't enlarge on this further. It's many a year before another war can possibly take place, and it's now a waste of educated labour to discuss it further."

## A CONSTITUTIONAL POINT

Yet the constitutional question involved is one of vital importance. Besides Admiral Oliver, Lord Fisher and Sir Arthur Wilson were the only naval members of the War Staff Group. It comes, therefore, to this: Was the War Staff Group to be treated as cavalierly as the Board itself? Was it to be ignored unless it shared the views of the First Lord? Such in effect would appear to have been Mr. Churchill's opinion.

**The First Lord seems to have acted throughout as though the office of Lord High Admiral had been revived in his own person.**

He seemed to imagine that he was at liberty to pick and choose his advisers as he liked. If one Admiral did not agree with him, he looked for some other who did. Even so, he accepted only so much of the advice proffered as suited him.

On May 14 he wrote quite frankly to the Prime Minister that, in certain eventualities, he intended to act entirely on his own responsibility. "A moment," he said, "will probably arise in these operations (Gallipoli) when the Admiral and the General on the spot will wish and require to nm a risk with the Fleet for a great and decisive effort. If I agree with them, I shall sanction it, and I cannot undertake to be paralysed by the veto of a friend who whatever the result will certainly say, 'I was always against the Dardanelles.'"[39]

The next day Lord Fisher resigned and incidentally settled the

---

An article signed "Flag Officer" appeared in the October 1925 number of *The National Review* describing, in some detail, Mr. Churchil's high-handed methods at the Admiralty. (P.N. we have reproduced it as an appendix. It is possible that the article was written by the author.)
39      *World Crisis*, 1915, p. 354.

fate of the First Lord and of the Liberal Government.[40]

## DISREGARD OF EXPERT ADVICE

The view that Mr. Churchill disregarded throughout the views of the experts is strengthened by much that occurred at the War Council's meetings. On this point the verdict of the Commission is conclusive.

"There can be no doubt," it is stated,[41] "that at the two meetings on January 28, Mr. Churchill strongly advocated the adoption of the Dardanelles enterprise. When Sir Arthur Wilson was asked 'Did the First Lord express an opinion in favour of it ?' he replied 'Yes, very much! He pressed it very strongly.' We think that, considering what Mr. Churchill knew of the opinions entertained by Lord Fisher and Sir Arthur Wilson, and considering also the fact that the other experts at the Admiralty who had been consulted, although they assented to an attack on the Outer Forts of the Dardanelles and to progressive operations thereafter up the Straits as far as might be found practicable, had not done so with any great cordiality or enthusiasm, he ought, instead of urging Lord Fisher, as he seems to have done at a private meeting after luncheon on January 28 to give a silent, but manifestly very reluctant, consent to the undertaking, not merely to have invited Lord Fisher and Sir Arthur Wilson to express their views freely to the Council, but further to have insisted on their doing so, in order that the Ministerial members might be placed in full possession of all the arguments for and against the enterprise.

"We have not the least doubt that, in speaking at the Council, Mr. Churchill thought he was correctly representing the collective views of the Admiralty experts. But, without in any way wishing to impugn his good faith, it seems clear that he was carried away by his sanguine temperament and his firm belief in the undertaking which he advocated.

"Although none of his expert advisers absolutely expressed dissent, all the evidence laid before us leads us to the conclusion that Mr. Churchill had obtained their support to a less extent than he

40      Mr Churchill, though he ceased to be First Lord of the Admiralty in May, remained a member of the Committees which conducted the Gallipoli campaign. When in November evacuation was seen to be inevitable, he resigned office and left the Government.
41      D.C. I. 92.

himself imagined."

As confirming the view that expert opinion did not carry much weight at the Admiralty during the period under review, we have the evidence of the Marquis of Milford Haven who, as Prince Louis of Battenberg, had been First Sea Lord till the end of October 1914.

He is represented by Lord Bertie, the British Ambassador in Paris, as telling him that "Churchill did not act on expert opinions. He chose to think that he, a civilian, knew more about naval and military possibilities than the experts. * * * (publisher note: these are original *author's emphasis*)

"He had actually given orders for an immediate bombardment without consulting any of the Board as to the utility or feasibility of that particular bombardment."[42] Presumably the unfortunate bombardment of the Outer Forts of the Dardanelles on November 3, 1914, mentioned in the previous chapter, is the incident alluded to.

## THE FIRST LORD'S POWERS

The foregoing description of the position and powers assumed by the First Lord of the Admiralty in 1915, and of his relations with his experts, has not been written out of any desire to stir up past controversies, still less to attack an individual Minister now holding a high position, or to provide mere sensational reading.

As will be explained later on, constitutional problems of the utmost importance are involved, and for this reason all that Mr. Churchill said and did during the period that the naval attack against the Dardanelles was under consideration has to be closely examined and criticised. His relations with the War Council, with the Board of Admiralty, with the War Staff Group and the naval experts generally, with the Admirals in command of fleets, and with his colleague the Secretary of State for War are, from the constitutional point of view, all matters of first-rate importance. Questions of principle are raised which cannot be allowed to remain longer in abeyance.

It is certainly arguable that Mr. Churchill, in acting as he did, was fully within his rights as First Lord. The role he assumed was

---

42      Lord Bertie's *Diary*, vol. ii. p. 148.

practically identical with that played by Lord Kitchener at the War Office.

**Both acted as de facto Commanders-in-chief as well as Secretaries of State; both combined in their own persons powers of command and of administration.**

Herein lies one of the greatest, if not the greatest, lesson of the whole war.

Accordingly, the story of the events which led up to the naval attack on the Dardanelles fortress has to be told faithfully and without regard to personal considerations. Unless it is, the true history of the Dardanelles-Gallipoli campaign will never be understood, and, without the truth, the nation and the Empire will never grasp the extent of the dangers they run in war, not merely from without but also from within.

# CHAPTER IV

# THE SHORT CUT TO VICTORY

THE Cabinet room at 10 Downing Street must in its time have witnessed many a strange scene, but it may be doubted whether it ever looked on one more curious or more dramatic than that which occurred on January 28, 1915. On this day the Council, to which the war destinies of the nation were confided, met there to decide a matter in which the lives of thousands, the expenditure of countless millions of treasure, possibly the fate of the whole war, were to be involved.

Before the meeting Mr. Churchill and Lord Fisher met in the Prime Minister's room and discussed with him the memoranda of January 25 and 27 referred to in the previous chapter. The Prime Minister, after hearing both sides, expressed his concurrence in Mr. Churchill's views.[43]

Mr. Asquith's frame of mind at this time can best be understood by a reference to the evidence he gave later before the Dardanelles Commission. We know already that he assumed, quite wrongly, that the First Lord was speaking with the authority of the Board of Admiralty behind him. Further, on being asked in what light he interpreted the views of the experts, he replied: "Very favourable. Mr. Churchill told me so, and I thought they were. . . . Lord Fisher would always have preferred a conjoint military and naval operation, but he never said the Dardanelles expedition was doomed to failure; and I do not think he thought it was."[44]

It is to be observed that Lord Fisher's memorandum was not in the hands of the Council when the meeting took place, nor were they informed of the conversation which immediately preceded it.[45]

At 11.30 A.M. the Council met. "Mr. Churchill," so runs the record of the proceedings as given in the report of the Commission,[46] "said that he had communicated to the Grand Duke Nicholas and to the French Admiralty the project for a naval attack on the Dardanelles. The Grand Duke had replied with enthusiasm,

43    D.C. I. 85.
44    D.C. I. 68.
45    D.C. I. 87.
46    D.C. I. 86.

and believed that this might assist him. The French Admiralty had also sent a favourable reply, and had promised co-operation. Preparations were in hand for commencing about the middle of February. He asked if the War Council attached importance to this operation, which undoubtedly involved some risk.

"Lord Fisher said that he had understood that this question would not be raised to-day. The Prime Minister was well aware of his own views in regard to it. The Prime Minister said that, in view of the steps that had already been taken, the question could not well be left in abeyance."

About this time a dramatic scene occurred, which is thus described in Lord Fisher's "*Memories*" (p. 59). "Lord Fisher sat and listened to the men who knew nothing about it and heard one after another pass opinion in favour of a venture to which he was opposed. He rose abruptly from the table and made as if to leave the room.

"The tall figure of Lord Kitchener rose and followed him. The two stood by the window for some time in conversation and then both took their seats again. In Lord Fisher's own words: 'I reluctantly gave in to Lord Kitchener and resumed my seat.'

"Mr. Asquith saw that drama enacted, and Mr. Asquith knew that it arose out of Lord Fisher's opposition to the scheme under discussion. But he allowed his colleagues on the Council to reach their conclusions without drawing from the expert his opinion for their guidance. The monstrous decision was therefore taken without it. But they all knew it— such a scene could not occur without everyone knowing the cause."

Parenthetically, the reasons given by Lord Fisher himself for succumbing must be mentioned. "Lord Kitchener," he writes," was so earnest and even emotional that I should return that I said to myself after some delay, 'Well, we can withdraw the ships at any moment, so long as the Military don't land.'" He adds that he was mad on the Armada of 612 vessels, on which the success of his own North Sea Baltic scheme depended.

In his own words: "He was very largely influenced to remain because he was convinced it was of vital importance to the nation to carry out the large building programme initiated by him, which was to enable the Navy to deal such a decisive blow in the decisive theatre (in northern waters) as would shorten the war."[47]

To resume. The further official record of the meeting is as follows:

"Lord Kitchener considered the naval attack to be vitally important. If successful its effect would be equivalent to that of a successful campaign fought with the new armies. One merit of the scheme was that, if satisfactory progress was not made, the attack could be broken off.

"Mr. Balfour then dwelt on the advantages which would accrue from a successful attack on the Dardanelles, and concluded by saying that 'it was difficult to imagine a more helpful operation.'

"Sir Edward Grey said it would also finally settle the attitude of Bulgaria and the whole of the Balkans.

"Mr. Churchill said that the Naval Commander-in-Chief of the Mediterranean had expressed his belief that it could be done. He required from three weeks to a month to accomplish it. The necessary ships were already on their way to the Dardanelles."

So much and no more is the official record of this historic meeting. Fortunately, however, evidence quoted by the Commission in their Report throws further light on what occurred.

Take, for example, the following extracts[48] from Sir Arthur Wilson's evidence:

"Q. In the discussions prior to January 13, leaving the First Lord out, was there any general consensus of naval opinion favourable to an exclusively naval attack? A. I do not think there was.

"Q. In representing the opinion of the Admiralty to the War Council on the 13th January, or on the 28th, did the First Lord reflect these unfavourable opinions? A. No. I think he rather passed them over. He was very keen on his own views.

"Q. In what way did you think the First Lord failed to represent the difficulties to the War Council ? A. In the first place, he kept on saying he could do it without the Army; he only wanted the Army to come in and reap the fruits, I think, was his expression; and I think he generally minimised the risks from mobile guns, and

---

47    *Memories*, p. 67.
48    D.C. I. 88.

treated it as if armoured ships were immune altogether from injury. I do not mean to say he actually said they were immune, but he minimised the risk a great deal."

After reading such evidence surprise can hardly be felt that the Commission recorded its opinion of the Council's discussions in the following terms:

"What actually happened was that the stress laid upon the unquestionable advantages which would accrue from success was so great that the disadvantages which would arise in the not improbable case of failure were insufficiently considered."[49]

Mr. Churchill's description of a later phase of the Council's deliberations must be held to apply with equal, if not greater, force to the proceedings of January 28. "So obliquely," he says, "were these issues presented, so baffling were the personal factors involved, that the War Council was drawn insensibly and irresistibly into the gulf."[50]

Before leaving the proceedings of the meeting of January 28 one astounding fact must be emphasised to the full extent of the printer's powers.

**What was represented as a purely naval problem was under discussion. At the table sat two of the most distinguished sailors of the day, both of them Admirals of the Fleet. Neither was asked to express an opinion, and neither did so. Admittedly both would have voted against the scheme had a vote been taken.**

No amount of argument or casuistry can ever gainsay this one amazing fact.

## AMATEUR AND EXPERT

The reader is asked to pause for a moment and consider the inner meaning of these proceedings. The War Council consisted of very distinguished and very able men who doubtless could have formed an excellent judgement on the admissibility of any strategical project, had it been fully and fairly explained to them in the proper light and in all its bearings. Political considerations, internal as well as external, were bound to enter into the problem, and on such matters they were better judges than either sailors or soldiers.

49      D.C. I. 93.
50      World Crisis, 1915, p. 172.

But sight must never be lost of the fact that they were all of them amateurs so far as naval warfare was concerned. Not one had, either by long experience or by specialised study of strategy, acquired instinctive knowledge of what in any given situation could, or could not, be done.

To revert for a moment to the chess analogy, Mason in his "*Principles of Chess*" makes the following pregnant remarks:

"Submit even the most complex of problems to a dozen skilful players, and there will be no difference of opinion as to the proper course of procedure from first to last.

"They agree directly as to what is best to be done, and carry on the winning play without hesitation, even though none of them have seen that particular position before.

"They will see at once that something is to be done: their general knowledge of Chess will suggest what that thing must be."

So it is with the experienced and instructed sailor or soldier. He recognises intuitively what in any given situation ought to be done, and what must be avoided. His acquired instinct shows him things that are hidden from the tyro and the amateur.

**The problem on which the War Council was asked to decide should, as has been already explained, have been presented to it as a military problem and not as a naval problem.**

Had half a dozen sailors and soldiers been assembled, and had the question of Turkey's defeat been submitted to them, so much would have been established in half an hour's discussion. In fact, this very problem of attacking the Dardanelles had, a few years previously, been discussed conjointly by the naval and military staffs, and the military view that such an attack was not a feasible operation of war had then prevailed. Had it again been discussed in a similar manner, by soldiers and sailors left to themselves, the conclusion arrived at would inevitably have been the same.

But this very problem was now put before the Council as a purely naval problem. Mr. Churchill "kept on saying he could do it without the Army."

# THE PLAN

The strategical plans which were in the minds of Lord Kitchener and Lord Fisher in January 1915 have already been described. The plan now advocated by the First Lord was simplicity itself. The British fleet at the Dardanelles was gradually to destroy by gunfire the seaward forts of the fortress, sweep up or break through the mine-field known to exist in the narrow waters south of Chanak,[51] sail through the Straits, some 40 miles in length, which connect the Aegaean with the Sea of Marmora, and approach Constantinople, engaging en route the *Goeben* and the *Breslau* and the rest of the Turkish fleet if they were encountered.

On the fleet's arrival at the Turkish capital a revolution was to take place and the Ottoman Government was to sue for terms of peace.

**Without a revolution the whole plan was bound to fail. To this extent it was a pure gamble.**

The following questions are, therefore, pertinent. Was a revolution likely to occur? If it did not, what would have been the situation of the victorious fleet?

The fleet, as we know, never reached even the Intermediate Defences of the fortress, and accordingly what would have happened if a passage had been forced is largely a matter of conjecture. What we do know is that the Sultan, the Government (for all practical purposes Enver Pasha) and the central army of reserve were, in the event of an Allied success, to abandon the capital and withdraw into Asia Minor. In these circumstances a revolution depended on the Turkish Army mutinying and refusing to obey orders. But a mutiny in the presence of an enemy is an unlikely event, especially when a nation, as was the case with the Turks in 1915, knows it is fighting for its national existence. History records very few examples of such a breakdown of military discipline.

Accordingly the underlying idea of the whole plan was Utopian in the extreme.

---

51      It is now known that there were ten lines of mines, or 324 mines in all, in the narrow space between Chanak and the Intermediate Defences (*The World Crisis*, 1915, p. 260).

# THE LESSON OF 1922

Failing a mutiny, the probable course of events is no longer a matter of hypothesis. We know now from bitter experience what the position of the fleet would have been, after it had been a short time in the Marmora.

In 1922 Allied forces held Constantinople and were entrenched on both sides of the Bosphorus. A powerful fleet was in the Marmora and British troops were in full possession of the Gallipoli Peninsula and of the hills round Chanak. Mustapha Kemal, having behind him an army nothing like so numerous or so well equipped as Enver commanded in 1915, had defied the Allies from Angora, and war at one time seemed imminent.

Had it supervened, there is not the least doubt but that the whole of the Allied forces of occupation, naval as well as military, would have been placed in a situation of the greatest difficulty. Unless the Powers represented were prepared at short notice to put in the field armies sufficiently numerous to crush Turkish resistance, the best that could be hoped for was that their detachments then in Turkey could be withdrawn without a serious military disaster occurring.

The fleet, it is true, might have continued for a while to dominate Constantinople with little danger to itself, but a few guns of position, placed by the enemy anywhere on the Asiatic coast opposite the Gallipoli Peninsula, would have effectually prevented a single supply or store ship reaching it. It, too, must have abandoned the Marmora.

If, in February or March 1915, our fleet had reached Constantinople, and if the Turkish army had remained staunch, the same thing would have happened.

Admiral Jackson's prognostications in his memorandum of January 5 would certainly have been fulfilled. Like Admiral Duckworth's squadron in 1806, those of our battleships that had survived the forcing of the Straits would, after a short interval, have had to fight their way out again as best they could.

**In the face of an undefeated Turkish army no fleet could remain for long in the Sea of Marmora. The problem throughout was military and not naval.**

From whatever standpoint the naval attack on the Dardanelles

fortress is viewed, whether of the hopeful plans it supplanted, or of
its very speculative character, or of the misuse of naval power, or of
the naval risks involved and the losses entailed, or, not least, of its
false objective, as a strategical conception it stands self-condemned.

## THE DECISION

Such in broadest outline was the plan on which the War Council,
after a few hours' perfunctory discussion, was asked to register a
decision. Its members, most of them very busy men, had to guide
them only the explanations of a civilian Minister who "was very
keen on his own views," who "minimised the risks," who rather
passed over unfavourable opinions, and who stated definitely that
"he could do it without the Army."

Hence, of course, Lord Kitchener's acquiescence and his persua-
sion of Lord Fisher to resume his seat. Naval action, whatever the
result, could not but prove beneficial to the execution of the Alex-  ·
andretta project he had in mind at the time.

Hence, too, the Council's final decision come to at an evening
meeting on the same day (January 28). It was that—

**An attack should be made by the fleet alone with Constantino-
ple as its ultimate objective.**[52]

"This," said Mr. Churchill, "I take as the point of final decision.
After it, I never looked back. We had left the region of discussion
and consultation, of balancings and misgivings. The matter had
passed into the domain of action."[53]

Exactly so. All idea of abandoning the attack if it did not prove
successful, an argument which had carried so much weight with
the Council, was now thrown to the winds. So, too, as we are now
going to learn, were the assurances given that the assistance of the
Army would not be required.

**The matter had now passed into the domain of action. Amateur
strategy had triumphed.**

---

52      D.C. I. 90.
53      D.C. I. 89.

# CHAPTER V

# THE CATSPAW

The Gallipoli campaign will stand for all time as a classical example of disjointed action by a navy and an army, of national forces being thrown into battle piecemeal and being defeated in detail, of one service being dragged by the action of another service into an operation which proved its undoing.

In the interests of historical truth so much has to be said. It now becomes necessary to ascertain how so disastrous a clash of interests ever arose. Efforts have been made to prove that Lord Kitchener himself suggested the naval attack and accordingly must be held responsible for all its consequences. For example, in the official Naval History, by Sir Julian Corbett, it is asserted on p. 66 of Vol. II. that, in January, "as the result of a special study of this theatre (Turkey) by the General Staff, Lord Kitchener reached the conclusion that the Dardanelles was the most suitable objective."

Lord Kitchener, as we know from the findings of the Dardanelles Commission, asked only for a naval demonstration. Nothing more. Moreover, he had the Alexandretta project clearly in mind at this time.

As regards the alleged complicity of the General Staff, the assertion made can be proved to be incorrect. The two men who must have been charged with such a study—the Director of Military Operations (Major-General Sir Charles Callwell) and the officer who supervised the Turkish section (Brigadier-General Buckley)—are fortunately alive and able to speak for themselves. Both state positively that in January no such study was ever made by them or suggested to them. They affirm that it was not until the War Council began to discuss the question of military cooperation in February that Lord Kitchener directed them to explore the possibilities of military action in support of the fleet.

Further, there was the strongest possible reason why the General Staff should have been, and was, averse to any enterprise against the Dardanelles being undertaken. A joint discussion on this very project by the naval and military staffs has been already alluded to. This occurred in 1906, Lord Fisher being First Sea Lord at the time.

From the memorandum which issued as the result of this discussion it is clear that, although the naval authorities even then were in favour of a joint naval and military enterprise being attempted against the Dardanelles fortress, the General Staff would have nothing to do with it.

"The successful conclusion," so runs the memorandum,[54] "of a military operation against the Gallipoli Peninsula must depend on the ability of the fleet, not only to dominate the Turkish defences with gunfire and to crush their field troops during the period of helplessness which exists while an army is in process of dis-embarkation, but also to cover the advance of troops once ashore, until they could gain a firm foothold, and establish themselves upon the high ground in rear of the coast defences of the Dardanelles.

"In the opinion of the General Staff, a doubt exists whether the co-operating fleet would be able to give this absolute guarantee.

"However brilliant as a combination of war, and however fruitful in its consequences such an operation would be, were it crowned with success, the General Staff, in view of the risks involved, are not prepared to recommend its being attempted."

From this attitude the General Staff never receded. The Government of that day could not but be profoundly influenced by military opinion so strongly expressed. From 1907 onwards the idea of a Dardanelles venture was ruled out of account, and the decision then arrived at still held good down to February 1915.

Hard things have been said of the General Staff for not having ready prepared in their pigeon-holes a cut-and-dried scheme for the capture of the Dardanelles fortress. When, however, the facts of the case are known, they would more justly be open to criticism had they, after 1906, wasted their time and their exiguous secret service funds on an object which was no longer regarded as a feasible operation of war.

## 1906 MEMORANDUM IGNORED

In February 1915 the memorandum alluded to above was brought by the Prime Minister to the notice of the War Council who decided, however, to ignore its warnings. The reasons assigned

54      D.C. II. 10.

for the adoption of this course are as follows:

1.   The failure of the Turkish Army in 1911.
2.   Increased power of naval ordnance since 1906.
3.   The effect of the German heavy guns at Liége and Namur.
4.   Use of aircraft for "spotting" for the guns of the fleet.
5.   Turkish sea communications through the Marmora would be vulnerable to submarines.

When the decision to ignore the memorandum was arrived at, the naval attack had not yet begun and there were, therefore, some grounds for assuming that the doctrines of 1906 no longer held good in 1915. But long before the military landing took place in April, all these assumptions had either been disproved or had been proved to be of extremely doubtful worth.

The Turks had been fighting most stubbornly on the defensive; the naval gun, with its flat trajectory and armour piercing shells, had failed to silence the Inner Forts and had proved almost useless against entrenched troops and concealed artillery; for various reasons the seaplanes had been unable to render much assistance to the guns of the fleet; and, in spite of most gallant attempts, not a single submarine had reached the Marmora. It was in fact extremely doubtful whether the latter feat could be accomplished at all.

All these points had been brought to notice in the reports sent to London by the Admiral in command at the Dardanelles, so we have here a striking example of plainest warnings being set aside on grounds proved by experience to be wholly unjustifiable.

Had the Admiralty and War Ofiice staffs been kept in touch with one another, such things could not possibly have happened. General Callwell has affirmed more than once in his writings that, from January onwards, the two staffs were never given an opportunity of taking counsel together. Had naval and military experts met in conference to discuss the problem of the Dardanelles, he is convinced that both a naval attack and a military landing would have been ruled out as impossible undertakings.

# FEBRUARY 16

On January 28, as we know, the War Council had assented to a purely naval attack being directed against the Dardanelles Straits.

**Less than three weeks later, on February 16, the same Council decided to mass a considerable land force in the Mediterranean to be used as occasion might require. This force was to be available, in case of necessity, to support the naval attack on the Dardanelles.**

No adequate explanation has ever been afforded of this sudden change of front.

Nothing had happened to explain it. Not a shot had been fired by the fleet; the military position was still practically the same as it had been in January, when Lord Kitchener asserted with perfect truth: "We shall not be ready for anything big for some months."

The report of the Dardanelles Commission throws but little light on what happened between January 28 and February 16. All it tells us is that "after the meeting on January 28 the objective of the British Government remained the same, but the views entertained as to the means of realising it underwent a gradual but profound change. The necessity for employing a large military force became daily more apparent. The idea of a purely naval operation was gradually dropped. The prestige argument grew in importance. It does not appear that the Cabinet or the War Council ever definitely discussed and deliberately changed the policy. General Callwell says it would be very difficult to assign any date at which the change took place. 'We drifted' he said, 'into the big military attack.'

"At the evening meeting on January 28 Lord Kitchener had stated very plainly, in connection with the question which was then under discussion of affording assistance to Serbia, that we had at present no troops to spare. Mr. Churchill was of a different opinion."[55]

It seems not improbable that the clue to this mystery is to be found in the last sentence. On pp. 176-180 of his book, "*The World Crisis, 1915,*" Mr. Churchill tells us much that tends to enlightenment.

---

55      D.C. I. 95.

# MR. CHURCHILL'S ACTION

On January 29 and 30, at Lord Kitchener's suggestion, he interviewed Sir John French in France in the hopes of "procuring some military force to influence the political situation in the Balkans.[56]

" The Commander-in-Chief's view," he tells us, "was that the naval attack on the Dardanelles, on the practicability and technical details of which he could not pronounce, was in principle a most valuable and useful operation; but that any attempt at heavy military operations in the new theatre, such as would be entailed in the forcible occupation of the Gallipoli Peninsula, would be an altogether unjustifiable strain upon our military resources, and might lead to disaster either in France or at Gallipoli, through inadequate numbers and ammunition being available for both fronts.

"He was willing, however, to defer to the wishes of the Council by releasing in March, for political purposes in the Balkan States, two of the four new divisions which were to come to France."

"I was very much impressed," added Mr. Churchill, when reporting the result of this interview to Lord Kitchener, "with the Field-Marshal's desire to meet the wishes of the Government, even when he could not share our views."

Two things emerge from this incident. First, that on the morrow of the meeting of January 28 Mr. Churchill had the possibility of a Gallipoli landing clearly in view. Secondly, that in the two divisions Sir John French had offered to release there existed the nucleus of a force for an amphibious operation as opposed to a purely naval enterprise.

## NAVAL PRESSURE

One other thing is made clear by Mr. Churchill's own account. The naval experts, including Lord Fisher, who all along were "in favour of a combined attack, but not of action by the Fleet alone,"[57] continued to press their point of view urgently and incessantly. "Once it began to be realised that troops in considerable numbers were becoming available, Sir Henry Jackson and Lord Fisher began to press for their employment in the Dardanelles operation."[58]

---

56    *World Crisis*, 1915, p. 176.
57    D.C. I. 67.
58    *World Crisis*, 1915, p. 178.

"Lord Fisher was perfectly clear. He wanted the Gallipoli Peninsula stormed and held by the Army.

"I hope you were successful with Kitchener," he wrote to the First Lord on the evening of February 16, "in getting divisions sent to Lemnos to-morrow. Not a grain of wheat will come from the Black Sea unless there is military occupation of the Dardanelles, and it will be the wonder of the ages that no troops were sent to co-operate with the fleet with half a million soldiers in England."

On February 15 Sir Henry Jackson wrote a long memorandum[59] which was sent to Admiral Carden not as orders, but "as suggestions to be adopted by him or not at his discretion." It concluded in the following terms: "The full advantage of the undertaking (the naval attack) would only be obtained by the occupation of the Peninsula by a military force acting in conjunction with the naval operations, as the pressure of a strong field army of the enemy on the Peninsula would not only greatly harass the operations, but would render the passage of the Straits impracticable by any but powerfully armed vessels, even though all the permanent defences had been silenced.

"The naval bombardment is not recommended as a sound operation unless a strong military force is ready to assist in the operation or, at least, follow it up immediately the forts are silenced."

In view of the First Lord's assurances on January 28 that the Navy could act without the Army's help, comment on such "suggestions" seems superfluous.

Hardly less superfluous is comment on Mr. Churchill's own statement on the subject under discussion. "Amid the conflicting opinions, competing plans and shifting exigencies of the situation, the desirability of concentrating the largest possible army in the Eastern Mediterranean with extreme promptitude, and placing at its head a supreme general, seemed to us all at the Admiralty to be obvious. Therefore we at all times, in all discussions, supported everything that would promote and expedite this concentration."[60]

Enough has been said to show whence came the pressure which, in less than three weeks after an attack by the fleet alone had been decided on, induced the War Council on February 16 to register "

59    D.C. I. 95.
60    World Crisis, 1915, p. 180.

the all-important decision from which sprang the joint naval and military enterprise against the Gallipoli Peninsula."[61]

## THE ARMY CALLED ON

Without drawing on Sir John French's command, Lord Kitchener had at his disposal one division, and one division only, of seasoned and properly trained troops. This was the 29th Division, which in February was in process of formation in England. It was composed mainly of regular units withdrawn from overseas stations.

A bitter controversy soon arose as to whether this division should be sent to the Mediterranean or not. Its despatch was urged by the First Lord of the Admiralty and resisted by Lord Kitchener, who already had promised it to Sir John French. On February 19, 24, and 26, we are told, a series of "acute discussions" took place at the War Council.[62]

At the meeting on February 26 the First Lord formally recorded his dissent at the 29th Division being retained in this country, and added that "he must disclaim all responsibility if disaster occurred in Turkey owing to the insufficiency of troops."[63] Yet less than a month before, as Sir Arthur Wilson stated in his evidence, Mr. Churchill had "kept on saying he could do it without the Army."

Once again comment seems superfluous.

## THE ARMY'S RÔLE

One piece of evidence, fortunately preserved for posterity in the memorandum by Mr. Roch, which accompanies the Dardanelles Commission's report, makes clear much that might otherwise be obscure. Mr. Lloyd George, we are told, at the meeting on February 24 " strongly urged that the Army should not be required or expected to pull the chestnuts out of the fire for the Navy and that, if the Navy failed, we should try somewhere else, in the Balkans, and not necessarily at the Dardanelles."[64]

*Ex pede Herculem!*[65]

---

61      D.C. I. 96.

62      D.C. I. 99.

63      D.C.I. 101.

64      D.C.I. p. 56.

65      P.N. "from this foot we can measure Hercules," a maxim of pro-

This one piece of evidence, by itself, not only illustrates what went on at the "acute discussions" during February, but it also justifies fully the title given to this chapter.

## THE QUESTION OF PRESTIGE

One other fact of importance is stressed by the Dardanelles Commission. During February Lord Kitchener was becoming daily more impressed with the disastrous consequences likely to ensue if the Navy failed.

On February 24 he expressed the view that "if the Fleet would not get through the Straits unaided, the Army ought to see the business through. The effect of a defeat in the Orient would be very serious. There could be no going back. The publicity of the announcement had committed us."[66]

At first sight the last sentence is somewhat puzzling, as, on the date in question, nothing had occurred at the Dardanelles which committed us irretrievably. On February 19 the fleet bombarded the Outer Defences with indecisive results, and on February 22 a brief communique on the subject had been issued by the Admiralty to the Press.

But simultaneously a leading article, clearly inspired, had appeared in *The Times*, intimating in unmistakable terms that an attack of major importance had been opened, and that military assistance would be required.

In it the advantages, political, economic and military, of forcing the Straits were emphasised. The consequences of the fall of Constantinople, and of opening the way to Odessa, were touched on.

"The bombardment," the world was informed, "contains that touch of imagination which has of late been conspicuously lacking in the war."

"Bombardment from the sea," it was added, "will not carry such a project very far unless it is combined with troops.

"A bombardment of the entrance to the Dardanelles can only be satisfactorily developed into a combined land and sea attack, if the military strength employed is at least equivalent to the naval portionality and measurement attributed to Pythagoras. From a part we can know the whole.

66      D.C. I. 100.

strength.

"In other words it is not enough to have plenty of battleships, for plenty of troops are required also. The squadrons can do their part, but they must have an ample military backing. No greater mistake could be committed than to give the fleet insufiicient military support.

"The one thing that the Allies dare not risk in a persistent attack on the Dardanelles is failure.

"If the Peninsula of Gallipoli could be seized and safely held, the worst stage would be over!"

On March I another leading article appeared, headed "Forcing the Dardanelles," which was even more explicit as to our intentions. The presence of the *Queen Elizabeth* at the Dardanelles was announced; the news was stated to be extremely favourable and encouraging; and the success of the naval boat landings was emphasised.

The public were informed that "the moment a way is forced through the Dardanelles from end to end, Constantinople will be at the mercy of the Allied fleets." Once again they were asked to observe that "the attack is an example of far-seeing vision, of a kind which the Allies have so often lacked."

When reading these official announcements, for such in effect the articles amounted to, it must be borne in mind that the decision to break off the attack in the event of the fleet being unable to make headway still held good, and that the employment of troops was still under discussion in the War Council.

The article of February 22 would appear, in part at any rate, to explain what Lord Kitchener meant when, on the 24th, he stated that "the publicity of the announcement had committed us."

Moreover, both articles and another on March 5, entitled "The Dardanelles and After," give the key to what Lord Grey of Falloden had in mind when he wrote as follows: "The first attack appeared to have a great success, and the importance of the operation was at once boomed in a way that made it impossible to treat it thereafter as nothing more than a naval demonstration."****

"We stood publicly committed to an attack on the Dardanelles, as a serious effort, from which we could not withdraw, except by admission of a serious defeat. Kitchener was asked to provide troops for land operations in Gallipoli to support the fleet. This was the very thing that he had expressly stipulated that he should not be called upon to do, but in face of what had happened he could not now refuse."[67]

It will be for the historian of the future to analyse, and pronotmce on, the events towards the end of February 1915 which led directly to the military landing on the Gallipoli Peninsula. Some of those events have little to do with strategy, even amateur strategy, and the soldier has no desire to discuss matters which, fortunately, lie outside his province. He can only note the consequences of political action.

In this connection the following extract from Sir Ian Hamilton's "Gallipoli Diary" (p. 115) speaks for itself. Writing at Mudros on April 16, ten days that is before the landings, he remarks: "It is a huge handicap to us here that our great men keep all their tricks for their political friends, and have none to spare for their natural enemies. There has been very little attempt to disguise our aims in England."

Need more be said!

This only, perhaps. Following the publicity campaign in London, the Press in Egypt was permitted freely to announce the presence of the Expeditionary Force and discuss its destination. Gallipoli was clearly indicated.

**Never possibly has an enemy been given fuller warning of when and where to expect attack. Secrecy was ignored.**

## *LORD KITCHENER'S POSITION*

The dilemma in which Lord Kitchener was placed can only be described as tragic. He was under no illusion as to the task that would be imposed on the Army if the Navy failed.

At the end of February he sent General Birdwood from Egypt to report on the state of affairs at the Dardanelles, and from his reports he learned that the chances of naval success were uncertain, and that the defences of the Peninsula were of a very formidable

---

67      *Twenty-five Years*, 1892-1916, by Viscount Grey of Falloden, KG., vol. II. p. 76.

character.[68]

The information sent by General Maxwell from Egypt was even more specific. On February 24 he telegraphed that he understood that the Gallipoli Peninsula was everywhere heavily fortified and prepared for defence, and was practically a fort, advance against which from any quarter without heavy guns would seem to be hazardous.

Two days later Sir John Maxwell repeated to Lord Kitchener the views of Colonel Maucorps, a French officer, who had been for five years military attaché at Constantinople. His opinion was that it would be extremely hazardous to land on the Peninsula, which was very strongly fortified for defence. He estimated the garrison at 30,000 men under the command of an energetic officer.

Moreover, Lord Kitchener was fully aware of the large reserves in and near Constantinople. He could not have been insensible to the fact that he had neither trained men nor munitions, especially high explosive shells, sufficient for a fresh land campaign, which he knew from General Birdwood's reports early in March it would be impossible to restrict to minor operations.

But, in his mind, the idea of defeat in the East, and its possible consequences, overshadowed all other considerations. If the Navy failed, the Army must see the business through.

## SUBSEQUENT ACTION

On March 10 Lord Kitchener withdrew his opposition to the despatch of the 29th Division to the Mediterranean,[69] and on March 12 Sir Ian Hamilton was appointed to command a Mediterranean Expeditionary Force, estimated at 60,000 British troops, with a French division of colonial and native troops, about 18,000 strong. Of the British contingent only the 29th Division was adequately trained for offensive mobile operations.

On March 18 the combined French and British fleets attacked in strength the Intermediate and Inner Defences of the Dardanelles fortress. Of eighteen capital ships engaged three were sunk and three, including the modern battle cruiser *Inflexible*, were put out of action. There was no appreciable gain.

---

68    D.C. II. 12 and 13.
69    D.C. II. 17.

On March 19, in reply to a telegram from General Hamilton referring to the previous day's naval action, Lord Kitchener ordered military action in precise terms: "You know my views that the passage of the Dardanelles must be forced, and that if any large military operations on the Gallipoli Peninsula by the Army are necessary to clear the way, they must be undertaken, after careful consideration of the local defences, and must be carried through."[70]

## LOCAL CONDITIONS

The die was cast. The Army after all was to attempt to pull the chestnuts out of the fire for the Navy. An expeditionary force inferior in numbers and training to the armies the enemy could and did bring against it, without siege artillery save what the flat-trajectory guns of the Navy could supply, without bombs or siege paraphernalia, without any preconceived plan or previous preparations worth mentioning, without opportunity gradually to introduce new troops to active service conditions as was done on the Western Front, without a port of any sort to serve as a land base, was asked to assault a fortress that nature and man's efforts had combined to render well-nigh impregnable.

This, too, against German brain power and an enemy pre-eminently stubborn in defence, in a theatre where food and accommodation were non-existent, where the water supply proved totally inadequate,[71] where dysentery became epidemic and a plague of flies, loathsome and insanitary, rendered life intolerable, where the line of communication throughout was at the mercy of wind and waves and open to submarine attack, where room to manoeuvre, and even to form for attack, was wanting, and where every beach and every reserve position was under the direct aimed fire of the enemy's artillery.

As Sir John French had foretold in January, Gallipoli added to the Western Front strained our resources beyond the breaking point. Men and material proved insufficient for both campaigns.

In the striking words of an American writer, "the expedition remained to the end an illegitimate child, importunate in its

---

70      D.C. I. 114.
71      Tens of thousands of men and hundreds of mules subsisted for months on water brought in tankers from Port Said. This water was estimated locally to cost from 4*d*. to 6*d*. per gallon.

demands and annoying by the very fact of its existence."[72]

## THE MILITARY OPERATIONS

The sequel is well known. On April 25 landings were effected with heavy loss and a narrow foothold was gained ashore, which was held to the end. The attack, however, during eight months never succeeded in piercing the prepared outpost positions of the defence. The fortress's main line of defence was never even approached.

In August, after heavy reinforcements had been sent out from home, an attempt was made from the Suvla area against the fortress's land communications, but, like the earlier attacks against the fortress itself, it failed to effect anything. Partly owing to the inexperience of the troops employed, but mainly to the enemy still having considerable reserves in hand, this attack was soon brought to a standstill, and months of heart-breaking trench warfare followed.

The enterprise so reluctantly begun was as reluctantly abandoned. On October 31 General Monro, who had been sent out from home to command the expeditionary force and to inform the Government on the situation, reported definitely in favour of evacuation.

The Cabinet in London, being still unconvinced, invited Lord Kitchener to visit the Peninsula and state his views. On November 15 he pronounced strongly in favour of evacuation, but procrastination still continued and thousands of lives were uselessly sacrificed in consequence. It was not till December 7 that orders for withdrawal were issued by the Government, and it was not till January 8, 1916, that the last man left the Peninsula.

## THE CAMPAIGN REVIEWED

Attempts have been made to justify this campaign on the score that, during its course, the flower of the Turkish army was contained and decimated. That this happened is true, but similar results could have been attained at many points elsewhere, at Alexandretta in particular, with less effort to ourselves and at far less sacrifice of men, money, and shipping.

For the Turk land transport and supply have ever proved a source

---

72     Note by Major Sherman Miles, U.S. Army, in the U.S. Naval Institute *Proceedings*, June 1925, p. 1031.

of weakness in war, and the point selected for attacking him was just where his troubles in these respects were at a minimum and where our own were bound to be at a maximum.

Moreover, a policy of merely "killing Turks" was not the avowed object of the naval attack in the first instance or of the subsequent military expedition. A strategical plan must be judged on its merits and not by collateral issues or imagined consequences.

It was as a short cut to victory that the Dardanelles attack was designed, and it is as a short cut to victory that it must be judged. In this sense History is bound to pronounce it a dismal failure—a failure that is relieved only by the gallantry, the long-suffering and the patience of all—sailors, soldiers and airmen alike—who attempted the impossible.

Let it not be thought that a single word written so far implies, or is intended to imply, the smallest reflection on the conduct of the operations by the men on the spot, least of all on the naval and military commanders-in-chief. They did only what they were ordered to do; they did all, and more than all, that could reasonably be expected of them.

Responsibility for failure rests not with them but with those who, against expert advice and in the teeth of plainest warnings, embarked on an enterprise which, it is now clear, had from the beginning only the most slender, if any, prospect of success.

Few will be found to disagree with the following summary of this sad episode in our history, written by one who himself played a distinguished part in the Aegean in 1915.

"The campaign of the Dardanelles will remain through all ages to come an imperishable monument to the heroism of our race, to the courage and endurance of our soldiers and sailors, to the lack of vision and incapacity of our politicians."[73]

Admiral Wemyss fully endorses Mr. Page's scathing condemnation already quoted.[74]

One other thing requires in justice to be stated, and stated in the clearest terms. The Army bears no particle of ill-will against the Navy for its share in leading it into the Gallipoli shambles. There

73      *The Navy in the Dardanelles*, by Admiral of the Fleet Lord Wester-Wymss, p. 284
74      See preface.

was not an officer or man who fought and suffered on the Gallipoli Peninsula who did not realise that it was the ill-starred naval attack which had brought him there, but such thoughts never affected in the smallest degree the perfectly harmonious relations that subsisted between the two Services throughout the campaign. Never was brotherhood-in-arms more perfect or more cordial.

But, while excusing the Navy of all blame in the matter, the Army asks, and is entitled to ask, what the system of higher control was that made it possible for one Service to be played off against the other, and for sins of omission and commission to be perpetrated, which could, and would, have been avoided, had the directing staffs of the two Services been kept in close and constant touch, the one with the other, both before and during the war.

This question remains to be answered.

## CHAPTER VI

## SANHEDRIM CONTROL

"You cannot run war with a Sanhedrim,"[75] exclaimed Mr. Lloyd George in the House of Commons, when at the end of 1915 he became Prime Minister, and almost in the same breath he alluded to our having suffered disaster after disaster through tardiness of decision and action.

Unfortunately we are not told what were the deficiencies in the War Council, and its immediate successors in 1915 the Dardanelles Committee and the War Committee, that made Mr. Lloyd George, who was a member of all three, compare them with that eminently respectable body of high priests, scribes, pharisees and elders, which constituted the Jewish Council of State. It may have been a question of numbers; more likely it was a matter of qualifications or rather disqualifications. What is important is that, in the opinion of one who knew, the one Council was as unfit to be entrusted with the conduct of a great war as the other.

If any principle underlies the term "Sanhedrim Control" it is this, that sailors and soldiers must in all circumstances and under all conditions be kept in their places, and on no account must they be permitted to play any responsible part in the Nation's councils. The high priest, the scribe, the pharisee, and the elder, by virtue of his position as a member of a Sanhedrim, is fully qualified to deal with any question that arises, whether in peace or in war.

This is no mere fanciful supposition.

"The distinction between politics and strategy," so writes Mr. Churchill, "diminishes as the point of view is raised. At the summit true politics and strategy are one."[76]

Ergo, quite obviously, the politician is fully qualified to deal with

---

75      P.N. as noted before, this usage is meant as an organizational insight, not an ethnic prejudice. The Sanhedrin was a Jewish assembly of up to 70 priests and judges who administered the land of Israel. Lloyd George ran the war primarily through daily meetings of a Cabinet of Five, which he found more effective than larger councils. The author takes the Prime Minister's point and applies it to naval strategy.

76      *World Crisis*, 1915, p. 21.

strategy!

Hence Amateur Strategy!

Hence Gallipoli!

## POLITICS AND STRATEGY

It is well that this thesis that Politics and Strategy are one and the same thing has been so frankly stated. The ordinary man now knows where he stands and what the problem is with which he has to deal. For what is the meaning of such a claim?

If it means anything at all, it is equivalent to saying that every politician is a heaven-born naval and military strategist, that the man who produces a weapon is necessarily the right man to use it, that the administrator automatically becomes the commander.

**Politics and strategy are radically and fundamentally things apart from one another. Strategy begins where politics end.**

They connote different aptitudes of mind, wholly different training, and different methods of action.

No one knows this better than the sailor or soldier. The last thing he wants is to get mixed up in politics. He recognises that policy is the business of the politician, who provides and develops the national resources for war and decides against whom they are to be used.

All sailors and soldiers do ask is that, when policy is settled, the naval and military plans for defeating the enemy, *i.e.* Strategy, and the executive control of the forces provided to give effect to policy, *i.e.* Command, shall be regarded as being in a sphere apart from politics.

The politician, unfortunately, either cannot, or will not, recognise limitations in the scope of politics which ordinary common sense would seem to dictate. Only too often he trespasses on the purely military domain with disastrous consequences. Amateur Strategy and all it implies is the result.

## POLITICAL INTERFERENCE

On land the instances of political interference in the sphere of military strategy and command are too numerous and too notorious to need enumeration. One example will suffice. During the war between the United States of America and England in 1812-14, the American Secretary of War "issued orders in his own name governing the movement of the armies, and in every respect he held the generals in the relation of strict military subordination." One Secretary of War, a civilian, on one occasion actually assumed command in the field. During the civil war between the North and the South, similar interference on the part of the politicians was not unknown.[77]

"This union of the purse and the sword,"[78] to use the expression of the American historian, produced results quite as deleterious in the domain of administration as in the military sphere. The enemy alone benefited.

In naval matters, it must be owned, such interference on the part of the politician has been less common and less obtrusive. In our own country at any rate, the spectacle of a civilian Minister dictating naval strategy and acting in all respects as a naval commander-in-chief was unknown prior to 1914.

**It is a most ominous portent.**

## OUR SYSTEM IN THE PAST

Formerly in this country both the sailor and the soldier were, as regards the exercise of executive command, and in matters of honours and patronage, less subject to Parliamentary influences than they are to-day.

The Navy had its Board of Admiralty, con-sisting of executive officers who, as a Commission under the Crown, exercised the powers of the dormant office of Lord High Admiral. Its administration was vested in a separate Navy Board, the Board of Ord-

77      *The Military Policy of the United States*, by Major-General Upton, United States Army. (P.N. John Armstrong Jr. assumed command in New York and Washington D.C. He resigned following criticism when the capital was burned down, and was succeeded by James Monroe, who served as both Secretary of State and Secretary of War.)

78      P.N. the point here is that logistics and administration must be separate from strategic and tactical leadership. Dante makes a similar warning against the union of sword and crook i.e. church and state: "each has eclipsed the other; now the sword has joined the shepherd's crook; the two together must of necessity result in evil" (*Purgatorio* 16.109-111)

nance and other similar Boards, which functioned under powers derived directly from Parliament. Thus in former times the Board of Admiralty itself had no actual part in administration, and its members were free to apply their minds and their time to the consideration of war problems and to the conduct of operations. The Board constituted in fact what today is known as a Naval Staff, and it had full executive powers over the fleets.

Similarly the Army, as a result of William III's wise bargain with Parliament, had its own Commander-in-Chief, whose headquarters, at the Horse Guards, were quite separate from the Secretary at War's office in Pall Mall. The system which then obtained is thus described by Lord Haliburton, himself a great constitutional authority:

"The Commander-in-Chief was responsible to the King and the Government, but not directly to Parliament, for the efficiency of the Army, while the Secretary at War was directly responsible to Parliament for military expenditure and for the preservation of civil rights and privileges from military encroachment."

The predominant feature of this system was "the complete separation of command from the business administration of the Army."

"The Commander-in-Chief," remarked the Duke of Wellington, on a memorable occasion, "has and can have nothing whatever to say to finance. ... It is much better that the Secretary at War should be the person to regulate that matter."

Thus it is clear that, under the old system, the system that is of the eighteenth century and the Napoleonic wars, the distinction between command and administration, between the sword and the purse, was well understood both in the Navy and the Army, and that high authorities regarded with approval the maintenance of this distinction.

**During the nineteenth century, however, the lines of demarcation gradually disappeared.**

In 1831, for alleged reasons of economy, the Board of Admiralty and the Navy Board were amalgamated, and after the Crimean War the Commander-in-Chief's office was moved to Pall Mall, the Board of Ordnance was abolished, and the War Office, as we know it today, was gradually evolved.

# THE PRESENT POSITION

This brief historical survey has been necessary in order to make clear the present position of the naval and military expert in the body politic. Unquestionably the tendency in recent years has been to bring the executive command of both the Navy and the Army more directly under Parliament, and this tendency has become more pronounced as our form of government has become more democratic. The powers of the Cabinet Ministers, who preside at the Admiralty and the War Office respectively, have increased beyond measure in matters pertaining to command, honours and patronage. Herein, without question, lies a great danger.

"If," said Lord Palmerston more than one hundred years ago, "the day came when the power of rewarding military services should be transferred from the Crown to the House of Commons, those who saw it might say that they had witnessed the death blow to the Constitution."

When the Great War came, almost every vestige of constitutional distinction between command and administration had disappeared, not in the Army alone, but in the Navy as well. As already pointed out:

**Both the First Lord and the Secretary of State for War became de facto Commanders-in-chief of the fighting forces of the Crown. They combined in their own persons full powers both of command and of administration.**

This fact is of supreme national importance and deserves attention on its merits, apart altogether from the personalities of the men who, in 1915, held the posts in question.

Had a civilian been Secretary of State for War in 1915, his latent powers would have been just as great as those exercised by Lord Kitchener. How he acted would have depended on his own good sense and judgement.

When attending War Council meetings his experts would have been in precisely the same position as were Lord Fisher and Sir James Wolfe Murray, and to a certainty they would have acted as they acted. Human fallibility cannot be counted on to resist influences that induced men like Fisher and Wilson to keep silence and sacrifice their convictions.

## POSITION OF THE EXPERT

There is more behind Sanhedrim control than mere constitutional proprieties. The personal factor cannot be ignored. For example, let us examine somewhat closely the feelings of a sailor or soldier who is invited by his Minister to accompany him to a Cabinet, or Cabinet Committee, meeting, to advise on plans or technical questions of the highest importance.

As matters stand, it is probably due to the Minister's influence that he holds the position he does, and to that extent he is under a sense of obligation to him. In any event a sense of loyalty to his chief, a characteristic which a lifetime spent in either Service implants firmly in a man, precludes him from (in Lord Fisher's picturesque phraseology) kicking his Minister's shins at the Council table.

There is also another and less worthy motive for acquiescence with the Minister's views. Should the expert express unpalatable opinions he cannot but realise that his future prospects are apt to be prejudiced. He may come to be regarded as a "difficult" person who had better be sidetracked. While human frailty exists, can real independence of expression be looked for in such circumstances?

But even assuming that the expert is the most independent of men, not only in character but also as touching his worldly possessions, he is still handicapped from the start by the atmosphere in which he is called on to express his views. He is introduced into a fairly numerous assembly of Cabinet Ministers who are all more or less trained rhetoricians and dialecticians. The expert is neither.

"When sailors get round a Council Board," writes Lord Fisher,[79] "they are almost invariably mute. The Politicians who are round that Board are not mute; they never would have got there if they had been mute. That's why for the life of me I can't understand what on earth made David say in the Psalms 'A man full of words shall not prosper on the Earth.' They are the very ones who do prosper."

In his evidence before the Dardanelles Commission, Lord Crewe made the following significant statement: "The political members of the War Council did too much of the talking and the expert

---

79     *Memories*, p. 61. (P.N. with allusion to Psalm 140)

members as a rule too little."[80]

In fact our independently-minded expert has everything against him. He is probably bad at expressing himself, and if anything in the nature of a debate arises he is no match, and he knows it, for men to whom debate is as the very breath of their nostrils. There have been men in the past like Field-Marshal Lord Nicholson, for instance, to whom such a consideration would not apply, but such men are the exception rather than the rule.

## HIS CONSTITUTIONAL STATUS

Moreover, the expert, if he hold an official position, may be in doubt as to his constitutional status in so august an assembly as a War Council which, as is explained later, was for all practical purposes a Cabinet Committee, wielding the full powers of the Cabinet. This matter is discussed at length in the report of the Dardanelles Commission, and various opinions are expressed regarding the silence of the experts. But there can be little doubt that the view of their position held by both the First Sea Lord and the Chief of the Imperial General Staff was, as matters stood in January and February 1915, constitutionally the correct one.

**Silence or resignation was their only alternative.**

Sir Arthur Wilson who, though holding no official position, was specially invited to attend the War Council meetings, was differently situated. He was one of the most independently minded of men and explained his silence in the following terms:

"I thought other things might be better, but both the First Lord and I recognised that it was not my business to interfere and if they (the Council) decided on a plan all I was to do was to help them to the best of my ability."[81]

Yet Sir Arthur Wilson was one of the two naval experts on whom the Council relied for advice and enlightenment, and whose silence was accepted as a sign of acquiescence in the naval attack on the Dardanelles. In the circumstances his presence at the War Council meetings was a snare and a delusion.

**As the experts did not express their opinions the Council was in technical matters guided wholly by the views laid before them**

---

80      D.C. I. 24.
81      D.C. I. 88.

by the First Lord of the Admiralty.[82]

## *A VITAL MATTER*

There is yet another reason, perhaps the most cogent of all, that causes the expert to keep his mouth tightly shut. A lifetime's training has made him averse to discussing before laymen matters of the utmost secrecy whose disclosure, however unintentional, may endanger the lives of thousands of his comrades. This is a delicate matter on which it is difficult for a soldier to write without giving offence.

Facts, however, speak for themselves.

**Lord Fisher, according to his own statements, shared his secrets with Sir Arthur Wilson and with no one else.**

Similarly, the Dardanelles Commission speak of the difficulty they found in faithfully representing, owing to his premature death, Lord Kitchener's aims and opinions.[83] "This difficulty," they say, "is enhanced owing to the strong opinion which Lord Kitchener entertained as to the absolute necessity of maintaining strictest secrecy in respect to all matters connected with military operations. Sir Maurice Hankey, indeed, stated that some difficulties at times arose owing to Lord Kitchener's unwillingness to impart full information even to the members of the War Council."[84]

Privately, to his intimate friends, Lord Kitchener expressed in strongest terms his reasons for such unwillingness.

To sum up: feelings of loyalty, want of skill in debate, his constitutional position it may be, and most certainly his ideas as to the vital need for secrecy are all factors which, combined, prevent the expert from giving full expression to his opinion at a Sanhedrim meeting, or indeed expressing any opinion at all. **Expert advice in such circumstances is apt to become, and in 1915 did become, a mere cloak for Amateur Strategy.**

---

82    D.C. I. 29.
83    D.C. 1.9.
84    Lieutenant-Colonel Sir Maurice Hankey was the Secretary of the War Council.

# CHAPTER VII

## PAST WARNINGS

SANHEDRIM control in war is nothing new in our history. The Royal Commission which, in 1903, reported on the events of the South African War arrived definitely at the conclusion that the conditions under which that campaign had been conceived and conducted were such as gravely to prejudice the chances of success. The conviction became prevalent that there must have been some radical defect in a system of higher control which could produce the happy-go-lucky methods which then prevailed.

Unfortunately, the nation at large has been left to this day in ignorance of the inner meaning of the South African lesson. Colonel G. F. R. Henderson, the talented author of the official history of that war, had, it is true, intended telling the story, with all its implications, especially in regard to the neglect of expert advice both before the war and subsequently. But pressure was brought to bear to prevent him from doing so, and what he had written of a political character was destroyed so effectually that it is doubtful whether a single copy of the chapters in question exists at the present time.

Certainly no man was better qualified to tell the truth than the late Colonel Henderson, than whom the Army has never produced a deeper thinker on war or a more brilliant writer. Had he been permitted to put his case plainly before the nation, a death blow would, in all human probability, have been struck at Amateur Strategy, and possibly, even probably, the Dardanelles-Gallipoli campaign would never have occurred.

## *THE ESHER COMMITTEE*

However this may be, the events of 1915 cannot be excused on the grounds that the lessons of the South African campaign were wholly neglected. In 1903 the Esher Committee was appointed to take action on the report of the Royal Commission. Lord Esher himself had been a member of the Commission, and, like many others, had been greatly impressed by the evidence given before that body.

The recommendations of his Committee may be said to have focused the chief lessons of the Boer War and, as far as political exigencies would permit, applied them in the reconstitution of the War Office which took place in 1904.[85]

Prior to, and during, the South African War the Commander-in-Chief was the sole military adviser of the Secretary of State and of the Government. Adequately to fulfil the multifarious duties pertaining to his high office, it had been pointed out by the Royal Commission that he required to be equally a master of administrative detail and a strategist and a trainer of troops of the first order. Theoretically, too, he was held to be the Inspecting Officer of all the military forces of the Crown.

**In view of such facts the Royal Commission had been unanimous in thinking that under modern conditions no man could be found with the mental and physical qualifications, to say nothing of the leisure or the training, required for so tremendous a task.**

In 1890 the Hartington Commission, which inquired into Army matters, had arrived at exactly the same conclusion.

In the first instance, therefore, the Esher Committee was faced with the necessity of redrawing the line of demarcation which formerly existed between purely administrative functions on the one hand and purely military functions on the other, and with making arrangements for the performance of either set of duties.

The abolition of the office of Commander-In-Chief, the institution of an Army Council on the analogy of the Admiralty Board, and the creation of a General Staff were all steps that proved to be necessary for the attainment of this object.

## A RESPONSIBLE EXPERT

A General Staff having been created, and the study of war problems and the preparation of the Army for war having been assigned as duties to its Chief, the next step was to ensure for him a position of responsibility in the conduct of war.

Here the Committee of Imperial Defence proved to be a *deus ex machina*. This body had been formed in 1901, on Mr. Balfour's

---

85     The author acted as secretary of the Esher Committee, so speaks with knowledge as to its aims and objects. (P.N. The Esher Report recommended radical reform of the British Army after the South African wars.)

initiative, to act as an advisory body to the Government in matters connected with war and defence. Under the Esher Committee's proposals, which were accepted by the Government, the recognised experts of the fighting services, **the First Sea Lord and the Chief of the General Staff, were in future to become ex-officio members of this body, and as members they would be bound to share unconditionally in the responsibility for advice tendered.**

Lord Esher and his colleagues, Sir John Fisher and Sir George Sydenham Clarke, conceived the Committee of Imperial Defence as essentially a body of experts, where sailors and soldiers, under the presidency of the Prime Minister, would be able to discuss together matters of interest common to both Services, and express their opinions freely, unhampered by the presence of numerous Cabinet Ministers.

In short, everything possible was done to ensure that the advice on war problems available for the Government should represent the bona-fide views of men who, by their training and special aptitudes, and owing to their having ample leisure for their task, should be fully qualified to advise and assist.

That this conception of the Committee of Imperial Defence was not realised and that gradually one civilian member after another was added to it until, prior to 1914, the political element outnumbered and too often out-argued the experts was not the fault of the Esher Committee. Had their recommendations been adopted in full and had the system they advocated been adhered to in 1915, one thing is certain. The want of touch between the naval and military staffs, the neglect of plainest warnings, the miscalculations of the enemy's and our own resources, the lack of considered plans, the improvised methods that were adopted, and other serious errors which marked the inception and the conduct of the Dardanelles-Gallipoli campaign, would assuredly have been avoided.

## EVENTS, 1904-1914

Subsequent events down to August 1914 amply justified the changes in system inaugurated in 1904. The salutary reforms effected during Mr. Haldane's administration at the War Office, the marked renascence of the military art during the years prior to the Great War, the successful despatch from these shores of the Expeditionary Force in August 1914, and not least the clear and emphatic warnings uttered by the General Staff against any form of military adventure on the Gallipoli Peninsula, can all be pointed to as the outcome of a system that had been adopted deliberately with a view to preventing in any future war a recurrence of the methods and unfortunate incidents that marked the opening phases of the Boer War.

In view of such achievements, it might seem natural that the Government would have been content to leave well alone and to continue in war a system which, in spite of certain imperfections, had already proved its efficacy.

## *1914-15*

But what happened?

**Within three months of war being declared every one of the safeguards introduced in 1904 to ensure that the best expert opinion should play a responsible part in the higher conduct of war had disappeared.**

**A system far worse than what had obtained in 1899, worse possibly than ever before in our history, was substituted.**

The collective responsibility of both the Board of Admiralty and of the Army Council disappeared, and neither the First Lord nor the Secretary of State for War spoke at the War Council with the sanction of their respective Boards behind them. The Chief of the Imperial General Staff was not even a member of the Army Council, and the usefulness of the General Staff suffered temporary eclipse during many months in 1915.

The Committee of Imperial Defence fell into abeyance in November 1914, and was replaced by a War Council which, though retaining many of its outward features, yet differed from it in matters of vital importance. The War Council met in the Cabinet Room at 10 Downing Street, not in Whitehall Gardens, the Defence Committee's home; it possessed supreme powers of decision which ordinarily pertain to the Cabinet alone; and its methods of procedure were quite different from those which obtained at a meeting of the Committee of Imperial Defence.

No agenda were circulated beforehand; the naval and military experts were no longer summoned in their capacity as members, but were merely invited by their departmental chiefs to accompany them; no shorthand reports were taken of its proceedings, and no minutes of discussions or of decisions arrived at were circulated to those who had been present at a meeting.

**War Council procedure was, in fact, much more akin to Cabinet procedure than to the Imperial Defence Committee's procedure.**

Hence arose the series of grave misunderstandings regarding the status of the expert advisers that have been referred to earlier— misunderstandings which unquestionably affected and gravely prejudiced the whole conduct of the war in the earlier days.

Most important of all, both at the Admiralty and at the War Office, the Cabinet Ministers in charge wielded autocratic powers as regards both command and administration, and became the sole advisers of the Government on the problems of the war. Every trace of the line of demarcation between executive and administrative functions was wiped out.

As a result there arose a state of affairs in every respect worse than that which had been so unsparingly condemned by the South African War Commission.

Whatever their aptitudes, neither Lord Kitchener nor Mr. Churchill, with all the other claims on their time, could possibly have had sufficient leisure to devote to the study of war problems, or to the reports received from the various theatres of operations, that close and undivided attention which alone qualifies a man to tender profitable advice or arrive at sane decisions.

As regards War Office procedure, the verdict of the Dardanelles Commission is identical with that of the South African War Commission. The result of the changes introduced after August 1914 was:

"To throw on the hands of one man an amount of work with which no individual, however capable, could hope to cope successfully"[86]

What applied to the Secretary of State for War applies with equal force to the First Lord of the Admiralty. Even had a sailor been First Lord in 1915, as Lord Barham was in 1805, it is certain that, under modern conditions, he would have found it impossible

---

86	D.C. I. 41.

successfully to combine the strategical and executive functions, now vested in the appointment, with its heavy administrative responsibilities, over and above his many Ministerial and Parliamentary duties.

Both in naval and in military affairs, the old distinction between command and administration is far more needed today than it was formerly.

## CAUSE AND EFFECT

A Greek dramatist would doubtless have attributed the War Council's decisions and in-decisions, which led step by step to the Gallipoli campaign, to the malign influence of some offended god or goddess.

Lord Fisher can only explain the phenomenon by saying that the Council was miasma'ed.

"It was a Miasma," he writes, "like invisible, scentless, and poisonous—*deadly* poisonous— gas that, to each of them on the War Council, floated down on them imperceptibly with rare subtle dialectical skill, and proved so incontestably to them that cutting off the enemy's big toe in the East was better than stabbing him to the heart in the West; and that the Dardanelles was better than the Baltic."[87]

The historian, however, has to look for some less recondite and more prosaic connection between cause and effect. This he is likely to discover, not so much in a study of human weakness, as by investigating the system under which the higher control of the Great War was conducted.

Like systems produce like results. What a Sanhedrim system of control had accomplished in South Africa in 1899, it accomplished even more effectually in the Aegean in 1915, and similar results it can always be counted on to produce if ever again it is attempted.

The questions, important beyond all others, on which the whole Empire has to make up its mind and unequivocally express its intentions are these:

**How in future is a Sanhedrim system of control in war to be avoided?**

**How is the qualified expert to be given a responsible position in the conduct of war?**

87      *Memories*, pp. 50 and 52.

# CHAPTER VIII

## THE PEOPLE'S SAFETY

"THERE are those who still insist on the omniscience of states-men; who regard the protest of the soldier as the mere outcome of injured vanity, and believe that politics must suffer unless the politician controls strategy as well as the finances."

As the late war made evident, these words remain as true to-day as they were when they were written many years since by Lord Wolseley, when introducing Colonel Henderson's masterly study of "Stonewall Jackson" to the public attention.

That work is indeed an epitome of the evils that spring from Amateur Strategy. "During the three years," it is there stated, "that the control of the armies of the North remained in the hands of the Cabinet, the balance of success lay with the Confederates."

**"But in March 1864 Grant was appointed Command-er-in-Chief; Lincoln abdicated his military functions in his favour, and the Secretary of War had nothing more to do than comply with his requisitions. Then, for the first time the enor-mous armies of the Union were manoeuvred in harmonious combination, and the superior force was exerted to its full effect."**

Taught by the stern logic of facts, the Republic of the North learned its lesson and courageously faced the issues. The command of its armies and its strategical plans were at long last removed from civilian control and placed unreservedly in the hands of an expert. From that moment the doom of the Southern States was sealed.

## *RÔLE OF THE STRATEGIST*

Politics must ever exercise a supreme influence on strategy, and politics are clearly the business of the politician. Interference by the sailor or the soldier in purely political matters like manpower, finance, and supply, is not less harmful than undue meddling by the layman in the regions of command and strategy. So much said, the need becomes patent for discriminating between the functions which, in war, properly pertain to the statesman on the one hand and to naval and military experts on the other.

As a preliminary to any discussion on control in war, a clear line of demarcation must first be sought for between politics and strategy. This line should be at least as distinct as that which used formerly to exist in this country between the functions of command and administration. In point of fact, the old practice would seem to indicate the path of safety for the future. Politics and administration are as clearly allied as are, or should be, strategy and command.

Such a grouping of functions is not only simple but is also natural. The qualities of mind and training which produce the administrator are not inconsistent with political understanding. On the other hand, the qualities which make for success in the domain of politics and administration are seldom found in the great masters of strategy. To quote modern examples only, neither the elder Moltke, nor Yamagata, nor Foch were administrators. All three eschewed politics and the methods of the politician. Not one of them would ever have consented to divulge his plans or dispositions to a layman.

"For war," wrote Lord Fisher in 1916, "you want a totally differently constituted mind to that of a statesman and politician. There are great exemplars of immense minds being utter fools! They weigh everything in the balance! I know great men who never came to a prompt decision—men who could talk a bird out of a tree!

**"War is big conceptions and quick decisions. Think in oceans. Shoot at sight! The essence of war is violence. Moderation in war is imbecility.**

"I could finish this present German submarine menace in a few weeks, but I must have POWER! My plans would be emasculated if I handed them in. I must be able to say to the men I employ: '*If you don't do what I tell you, I'll make your wife a widow and your house a dunghill!!!*' And they know I would."[88]

Here speaks the voice of genius—unhappily a voice crying in the wilderness. We can picture the old Admiral eating his heart out in exile in his Trafalgar Square office, believing firmly, like Pitt before him, that he, and he alone, could save the country from the dire peril that threatened its very fife in 1916; knowing too, that neither he nor any other man, however gifted, could prevail under the system of conducting war which then obtained.

88     *Memories*, p. 38.

The views he expresses so forcibly are but simple truth. Ability to conceive great plans, practical knowledge of ways and means, quickness of decision, swiftness in action, ruthlessness, and above all **secrecy**, are the qualities demanded in the individual, or individuals, on whom responsibility for the conduct of operations is laid.

**The strategist must have power commensurate with his vast responsibilities—power to plan without undue interference; power to advise freely, fearlessly, and as an equal; power to act swiftly, secretly and decisively.**

**POWER! In that one word lies the crux of the whole matter.**

Under a constitutional form of Government cannot means be found to confer on the expert, be he sailor, soldier, or airman, or, better still, on all three acting in combination, such a degree of power as will render their task a possible one? Policy without doubt must rest with some political authority, but, policy once settled, cannot its execution in war be left to the experts?

Is not the British Empire capable of doing as a matter of course what the American Republic did in its hour of need?

## THE PROBLEM

The simple problem to be faced is this:

**What is the most efficient method of conducting operations of war under a democratic form of government?**

Let it be clearly understood that there is here no question whatever of removing the conduct of war in its widest sense from the control of the nations which compose the British Empire. Each one of these nations must be free, in the future as in the past, to decide whether it will participate in any particular war, and the extent of its participation. But, given a desire to participate, how, when war supervenes, should the naval, military, and air forces of the Empire be controlled so as to **obtain from the start** their maximum effect?

## AN OBJECT LESSON

Possibly the nature of the problem can be best explained by an object lesson from our own history.

In July 1757 England's fortunes were at their lowest ebb. For more than a year she had been at war with France and, under a system near akin to Sanhedrim control, there seemed small prospect of her even muddling through to victory. Everywhere, by sea and on land, in Europe as well as in America, she had met with dire disaster.

"A despondency without parallel in our history took possession of our coolest statesmen, and even the impassive Chesterfield cried in despair, 'We are no longer a nation.'"[89]

Within the space of a few months the genius of one man, and the methods he adopted, had changed the whole aspect of the war and with it the course of history. Before the year 1759 had closed England, under Pitt's guidance, had laid, well and truly, the foundations of the British Empire, and incidentally of the American Republic. The events which led to this sudden change of fortune are writ large in the pages of history. So, too, are the qualities of the man who wrought the change.

For our present purpose, what needs to be emphasised are the methods of control which enabled Pitt to direct strategy and conduct war with such marked success.

## PITT'S METHODS

First and foremost he devoted all his time and energy to war problems, undisturbed by administrative worries.

**For the purposes of the war, we are told, "the administration was scientifically separated into a supply department and an executive department which were kept practically distinct."[90]**

Newcastle, the Premier, took supply; Pitt, his Secretary of State and the leader of the House of Commons, supervised the Navy, the Army, and External Affairs.

"Thus, without the preoccupation of supply, Pitt was free to co-ordinate the three national forces as completely and harmoniously as a general in the field wields his horse, foot, and artillery."

**"On this occasion we had for once an organisation for war which, theoretically at least, could scarcely be nearer perfection."**

Autocratic Pitt's methods certainly were. "I will be responsible for nothing that I do not direct," he told his colleagues of the Cab-

---

89   Green's *History of the English People*, vol. viii. p. 176.
90   Corbett's *Seven Years' War*, vol. i. p. 182.

inet. When a joint naval and military expedition was at issue he did not hesitate to issue orders, signed by himself, directly to the admiral and the general on whose cooperation success depended. But such procedure was the exception rather than the rule. Pitt never underestimated the value of expert advice, nor, when one Service alone was concerned, did he interfere unduly with the naval and military executives. Only when the cooperation of the two Services was at stake did he personally intervene.

Throughout the period of his triumphal progress Pitt leaned on two men of marked ability, Lord Anson the sailor and Lord Ligonier the military Commander-in-Chief.

**For practical purposes these three formed a triumvirate to conduct strategy and operations, Pitt the statesman and Foreign Minister being primus inter pares.**

## PITT'S THEORY

"Pitt," so Sir Julian Corbett tells us, "has afforded his country for all time, if she had the wit to understand, a complete system of how to use the peculiar strength that belongs to her and to no one else. Pitt's theory has found to this day no real resting-place in the English ideas of government." His theory, briefly stated, was this: that in the domain of strategy and of warlike operations, it is only by entrusting full and complete responsibility to one Minister, call him what you will, that a constitutional country can hope to wage war successfully.

**Under Pitt's system the activities of the naval and military forces were directed by one mind for a common object; plans affecting both Services were worked out jointly; preparations were carefully co-ordinated; rapidity in execution was attained; and, above all else, secrecy was assured.**

## A WAY TO SAFETY

Whatever may be said of Pitt's theory and methods, this much at least is certain, that their efficacy was proved in practice. We may, and probably will, be told that Pitt's system was unconstitutional and could not be tolerated in these more enlightened days. Any such argument, however, before it is accepted, deserves to be most critically examined by every thinking man and woman in the Empire.

It is they who, in the past, have suffered in their persons and in their pockets from the old British method of muddling through. It is they, too, who will similarly suffer in the future, if that method is tolerated any longer, not the politically minded gentlemen in Whitehall who are never called to account, no matter what blunders, or worse, they may perpetrate.

The wars of the future, like the last, will be national wars. More than ever civil populations will be brought within the zone of actual operations. Aerial warfare, in itself, makes this certain. It is probable, too, that, as a result of aerial warfare, the decision in war will be reached more rapidly in the future than in the past. The opening moves may well prove to be decisive.

Everything, therefore, must be ready and in working order. Improvised methods in gross and in detail must be ruled out of account. There can be no question, when war supervenes, of spending months, or even days, in casting about for a workable system of higher control whereby the whole forces of the Empire, by sea and land and air, may be coordinated and used to the greatest possible advantage.

If constitutional objections be raised to this or that plan that would make for efficiency, the answer is perfectly clear.

**A people's safety stands above constitutional theories.**

No one, least of all the sailor or the soldier, wants to see Prussianism or militarism raise its head in the Anglo-Saxon world. But there is a wide margin, a very wide margin, between militarism and Sanhedrim control in war.

"Even now after two centuries and a half," writes one who has made a special and invaluable study of British military history, "the vengeance of the nation upon the soldier remains insatiate and insatiable."[91]

Is this state of affairs to be continued? Is the sailor now to share the same curse that hitherto has rested on the soldier alone? Is the omniscience of the statesman for ever to be regarded as a fetish? Is the war expert always to remain in a helpless and irresponsible position?

The peoples of the Empire have had their lesson—a terrible and

---

91    *History of the British Army*, by Hon. J. W. Fortescue, vol. i. p. 257.

bitter lesson. It is for them to decide. Their safety and the safety of their children and their children's children are at stake.

***Salus populi suprema lex.*[92]**

---

92      P.N. "The wellbeing of the people is the supreme law." Cicero, *De Legibus.*

# CHAPTER IX

# A SUMMARY

ONE object, and one object only, has been kept in view hitherto: to explain a system of conducting war which rendered possible such an amazing state of affairs as is disclosed by the report of the Dardanelles Commission. But an equally astounding fact has still to be noted.

**Constitutionally our war system remains today exactly as it was in 1915. If war came tomorrow there is nothing to prevent identically the same things happening again as happened then.**

Cabinet responsibility in war matters, national and imperial, is still the same as in 1915. The Committee of Imperial Defence, in which the civilian element still predominates, goes on meeting and ruminating on defence problems. The latent powers of the First Lord of the Admiralty and of the Secretary of State for War are still those of a Commander-in-Chief as well as of an Administrator. Constitutionally, the Government must still "in technical matters be guided wholly by the views laid before them" by these two Ministers. Expert advice can still be accepted or ignored at will, as happened when the naval attack on the Dardanelles was under consideration.

The responsibilities of the Board of Admiralty and of the Army Council are unchanged, and the majority of their members are still engrossed with the daily routine of administration. An Air Ministry has, it is true, sprung into existence and, in so doing, has complicated the problem of coordination both in peace and in war. Otherwise everything remains just as we knew it before August 1914.

**And yet every one of these most respectable and respected peace institutions was found wanting and lapsed under the strain of war.**

The Cabinet delegated its powers to a body quite unknown to the Constitution; the Committee of Imperial Defence disappeared; no one can claim that the autocratic powers vested in the Navy and Army Ministers proved to be a success; for all the influence they exerted on the conduct of operations, the Naval and Military Boards might never have existed.[93]

## LESSONS OF THE WAR

The lessons of the Great War are so profound and so far-reaching that no Government has yet been found bold enough to tackle them wholesale. Departmentally, problems of tactics, of administration in the field and of war economics have been considered by committees, and books of regulation have been revised in the light of recent war experience.

Further, official war histories have been, or are being, written from which, however, all political matter of interest is carefully excluded. In this respect the story of the South African War history is being repeated.

But nothing done hitherto touches even the fringe of a vast network of problems which, sooner or later, must be faced.

## AN INQUIRY NEEDED

The appointment of a Royal Commission or Special Committee to gather up all the lessons of the war is unthinkable. The field is far too vast. But one problem, concrete, unmistakable and clearly defined, presses for solution. It is that propounded in the previous chapter:

**What is the most efficient method of conducting operations of war under a democratic form of government?**

In 1903, as a result of experience gained during the Boer War, an exactly similar problem arose touching the government of the Army, and, as already stated, a Special Committee under Lord Esher was appointed to consider it and make recommendations.

The Great War has taught us that not the War Office only, but the Admiralty, the Committee of Imperial Defence, even the Cabinet itself, must *as instruments for the conduct of war* be brought under review.

---

93      An impression exists that certain members of the Army Council went to France early in the war and that its usefulness was impaired in consequence. That was not the case. The Council remained after mobilisation exactly as it was before, Lord Kitchener only replacing Mr. Asquith as Secretary of State for War.

If the existing system failed, as it did fail, to coordinate the work of only two Services, much less will it avail to bring three into harmony.

**An inquiry into this most important matter is long overdue and should be insisted on.**

Vital interests common to the peoples of the whole Empire are at issue. It is for them, through their organs of the Press, to demand such an inquiry and eventually to see that the necessary steps to reform, no matter how drastic the proposals may be, are taken and, once taken, are adequately safeguarded.

## APPLICATION OF THE LESSONS

It is not within the scope of this volume to inquire at any length into the problem indicated or to prescribe remedies. But, in the light of what has been written in previous chapters, it may not be considered out of place, if, briefly and in summarised form, certain broad principles are suggested, which war experience points to as being sound and in accord with the dictates of common sense.

**In the first place a clear definition of functions is above all things necessary to salvation.**

A line of demarcation, as distinct as possible, has to be drawn between policy and strategy, between supply and operations, between the purse and the sword, between administration and command—fundamentally these groups of terms are synony-mous—and functions allotted accordingly. Separation of duties on these lines is not an impossible or even a difficult task.

What, however, will be difficult is to ensure that, when a solution has been found, both parties to the agreement will abstain in future from trespassing. The upas tree of Sanhedrimism has its roots more in the foibles of human nature than in a constitutional soil.

**Secondly, the line of demarcation advocated must extend from top to bottom, throughout every portion of the constitutional machine that has to do with the conduct of war.**

In the Committee of Imperial Defence, in the Cabinets of the Empire, in its Defence Ministries, including our own Admiralty, War Office, and Air Ministry, the distinction between politics and strategy, between the functions of administration and those of command, should be understood as clearly as they are with an army in the field.

We need not be terrified at the principle involved. It is purely British and democratic in origin, and, like many another British institutions, it has served to point the way in other countries when democracy has been at stake.

It was the product of our own Revolution of 1688. It was adopted in France, one hundred years later, at the time of her Great Revolution, and in practice it prevails there to this day. It is the principle which lay at the root of Pitt's theory and system, and it is the principle which Lincoln adopted in the hour of his country's need.

Short of autocracy, it is the only principle by which efficiency in war *from the start* can be assured. The alternative is Sanhedrim Control, Amateur Strategy and Muddling Through or Disaster.

**Thirdly, whatever system is considered necessary for war must be adopted and practised in peace.**

In all matters relating to war the argument must be from war to peace, and not vice versa. Any other method implies improvisation when war comes, and improvisation means time, possibly irretrievable time, lost at the start. The handicap is too crushing.

## IMPERIAL DEFENCE

If in the course of these pages little has been said regarding the Imperial aspect of the problems discussed, the omission is in no way due to the matter having been lost sight of. In point of fact, this aspect of the conduct of war stands in the foreground of the picture.

Nothing can be done without the cooperation and approval of the Dominions. They have suffered equally with ourselves from defects of system in the past. Equally with the Mother Country they are interested in securing that the work of the naval, military and air forces of the Empire is duly coordinated in peace, and that the conduct of war operations is placed in the hands of men trained for the business.

The Empire as a whole is vitally concerned in giving a death blow to Sanhedrimism and Amateur Strategy.

## A POSSIBLE SOLUTION

If, as seems likely, the Committee of Imperial Defence is to become a real Imperial Council for the conduct of war, and if, as seems desirable, that body is to be divided sharply into two Sections, one concerned with Policy and Means, the other with Strategy and Operations, it is the Cabinets of the Empire generally who must decide how the Council is to be constituted and what powers are to be vested in either of its two Sections.

Already Dominion statesmen have demonstrated that they will agree to any reasonable solution of the problem of defence. In 1907 they accepted the principle of a Military General Staff for the Empire as a whole, because—and the cause is noteworthy—Mr. Haldane (as he then was) was able to assure them that the essence of a General Staff is, that it is, as a body, divorced from active participation in administration.

The beneficial effects of the 1907 decision cannot be exaggerated. It is entirely due to that decision that the armies of the Empire entered on the Great War with a common doctrine of leading, training, and organisation.

Doubtless if Naval and Air Staffs come into being, divorced like the Imperial General Staff from active participation in administration and finance, they and their doctrines will equally be accepted by the Dominions. Should this happen and should, as would seem natural, the Heads of the three Staffs (drawn, it may be hoped, from any portion of the Empire) form the body of the Operations Section of the Committee of Imperial Defence, one part at least of the problem will have been solved.

If Pitt's theory, and it seems the only reasonable one, is adopted, some Minister acceptable to the whole Empire would then have to be nominated to act as the chairman of this Section. This done, only one thing would remain to be settled.

**The Empire as a whole would have to determine what executive powers shall be vested in the Operations Section the moment war supervenes, how such powers are to be exercised, and to what extent the Section is at liberty in peace to prepare imperially for war.**

Obviously the connection between the Policy Section and the

Operations Section of the Imperial War Council must be as close as possible, and the powers of the latter would depend to some extent on those inherent in the former. These, however, are matters beyond the scope of this volume to discuss.

This much, however, is certain:

If the peoples of the Empire will it, the problem of democracy producing a rational system for the conduct of war is not insoluble.

## A NOTE

*I crave indulgence if I end on a personal note. A few months since, standing amid the cemeteries of Gallipoli—the thirty-two great cemeteries which lie scattered from Suvla Bay to Helles Point—I resolved to tell the story of the events which, step by step, led to a land attack being launched against the Dardanelles fortress.*

*If that story was to be told at all, it had to be told fully, fearlessly and impartially. This I have endeavoured to do.*

*I now ask those who read to accept what has been written in the spirit which the men, to whose memory this volume is dedicated, would have wished : forgiving and forgetting past blunders, looking to the future without dwelling unduly on what is now beyond recall, bearing malice to none, determined only that the lessons learned at so tremendous a sacrifice shall not be lost in oblivion.*

*Individuals pass, systems remain. A system which produced a Gallipoli campaign cannot go unchallenged and unchanged.*

*If now the nations of the Empire will face with courage and determination the great issues that Gallipoli raises, their dead will not have died in vain.*

*Greek children standing by the bones of soldiers they have
collected, who died during the 1915 Gallipoli campaign, on
Hill 60, Anzac Cove in 1919.*

# Appendix A

## *The National Review*

## *October 1925, Volume 86, Issue 512*

## *Lest We Forget—The Tragedy of the Dardanelles*

## *by a Flag Officer*

"*So through a Churchill's excess of imagination, a layman's ignorance of artillery and the fatal power of a young enthusiasm to convince older and slower brains the tragedy of Gallipoli was born.*" (Concluding sentence of the Australian Official History of the War.)

Mr. Churchill, in his *World Crisis*, 1915, page 122, comments as follows: "It is my hope that the Australian people, towards whom I have always felt a solemn responsibility, will not rest content with a crude, so inaccurate, so incomplete, and so prejudiced a judgment, but will study the facts for themselves."

The present writer, though not an Australian, has accepted the invitation and has studied the facts for himself in the pages of the Report of the Royal Commission on the Dardanelles Expedition, in Mr. Churchill's book, *The World Crisis*, and by comparing what he saw with his own eyes and with what he has been told by eye-witnesses and actors in that great drama.

It may be asked why rake up this old story now? The answer is, because Mr. Winston Churchill is Chancellor of the Exchequer in a Conservative Administration which is entrusted by the people of this country the great charge of national reconstruction, and it is advisable that Mr. Churchill himself, his colleagues, and the general public should be reminded of what has gone before.

In any study of the Dardanelles campaign it is necessary to make a clear distinction between two separate operations, namely: (1) The forced entry into the Sea of Marmora through the Dardanelles of a hostile fleet in spite of the resistance offered by the fortifications of those Straits either fixed or floating; (2) the gaining of the control of the Dardanelles, Sea of Marmora, and Bosphorus, thereby giving free communication between the Mediterranean and the Black Sea. The latter operation involves the military occupation of both sides of the Dardanelles and of both sides of the Bosphorus.

It is proposed in this article to deal only with the first. Before doing so it is necessary to give a short description of the field of operations.

The Peninsula of Gallipoli, which is joined to the mainland of Turkey by the Isthmus of Bulair which is only three miles wide, runs south-west for a distance of over forty miles, widening gradually to a maximum of twelve miles about half-way, and then narrowing to a point at Cape Helles. It is separated from Asia by the Straits of the Dardanelles, which, extending from the town of Gallipoli to Forts Sedd-el-Bahr and Kum Kale at the entrance, a distance of between thirty and forty miles, have an average width of some two miles and are about one mile wide at the Narrows. Through these Straits there runs a constant current from the Sea of Marmora to the Mediterranean at about 2½ to 3 knots' speed in the main part of the Straits and increasing to as much as 5 knots at times at the Narrows. The land on both sides is mountainous, the hills rising to a maximum height of nearly 1,100 feet in the Peninsula and to over 3,000 feet on the Asiatic side.

In 1914 the Straits were defended at the entrance by two forts on the Peninsula and two on the Asiatic side. These mounted guns of from 6 to 11-inch calibre. The principal defences were at the Narrows—there were groups of forts at Kilid Bahr on the Peninsula and other groups at Chanak in Asia. Also advanced forts at Dardanos and White Cliffs in Asia, and at Soghan Dere and a spot to which no name is given opposite to Chanak. These had a number of guns up to 14-inch calibre.

The extent of the minefield was unknown, but it was obviously undesirable to take ships anywhere inside the Straits or into the approaches outside without first sweeping. As a matter of fact it extended from the Narrows to some way south of Kephez Burnu. The minefield in Erenkeui Bay, which caused the disaster of March 18th, was laid some days earlier.

The minefields at the Narrows and below it were protected not only by the forts but on either side of the Straits by a large number of guns and howitzers, scattered and well hidden, and powerful searchlights.

It was believed that torpedo tubes were fixed ashore at the Narrows.

To enable a fleet to pass through it was first necessary to destroy the forts at the entrance, sweep up any mine-fields there might be in the approaches, then sweep a sufficiently wide channel through the approaches to the Narrows, the Narrows themselves, and the Straits beyond, destroy or at least silence the forts and the other guns covering the minefields, deal with any torpedo tubes, and thus secure the passage of the ships destined to pass through.

In November 1914 Mr. Churchill first mooted the idea of an attack on the Dardanelles, but, as there were no troops available at the time, the project was dropped.

On January 2, 1915, a telegram was received from Petrograd, asking the British Government to make a demonstration in the Eastern Mediterranean in order to relieve the pressure the Russians were experiencing at the hands of the Turks in the Caucasus.

A survey of possibilities in the whole of the Near Eastern area led Lord Kitchener to the conclusion that the only means of doing this was by a naval demonstration against the Dardanelles, though he had very faint hopes that such action would afford any material relief to the Russians. A telegram to this effect was sent to Petrograd in reply.

Lord Fisher, on January 3rd, in a note to the First Lord, pointed out the futility of a demonstration by bombardment and outlined a plan:

I. Appoint Sir William Robertson, the present Quarter-master-General, to command the Expeditionary Force.

II. Immediately replace all Indian and 75,000 seasoned troops from Sir John French's command with Territorials, etc., from England (and as you yourself suggested), and embark this Turkish Expeditionary Force ostensibly for protection of Egypt with all possible dispatch at Marseilles, and land them at Besika Bay direct.
. . .

III. The Greeks to go for Gallipoli at the same time as we go for Besika, and the Bulgarians for Constantinople, and the Russians, the Serbians, and Rumanians for Austria (all this you said yourself).

IV. Sturdee forces the Dardanelles at the same time with *Majestic* class and *Canopus* class. God bless him!

But, as the great Napoleon said, "Celerity"—without it "Failure"!

In the history of the world a Junta has never won! You want *one* man!

On this Mr. Churchill, in his *World Crisis*, 1915, observes:

*There never was the slightest chance of the whole of the Fisher plan being carried into effect. Sir William Robertson, to whom he proposed to entrust it, would presumably have refused most strongly against it, his policy being concentration in the main, or, as he no doubt would have described it, the decisive theatre.*

*The withdrawal of the Indian Corps and 75,000 seasoned troops and their replacement by Territorial divisions would have been resisted to the point of resignation by the Commander-in-Chief supported by his whole staff. General Joffre and the French Government would have protested in a decisive manner. Lord Fisher's third paragraph about the Greeks, Bulgarians, Serbians, and Rumanians expresses exactly what everybody wanted. It was the obvious supreme objective in this part of the world. The question was how to procure it? This was the root of the matter. It was in connection with this that Lord Fisher's fourth paragraph made its impression upon me. Here, for the first time, was the suggestion of forcing the Dardanelles with the old battleships.*

*This series of weighty representations had the effect of making me reach the conclusion that I saw a great convergence of opinion in the direction of that attack upon the Dardanelles which I had always so greatly desired. The arguments in its favour were overwhelming, and now the highest authorities, political, naval, and military, were apparently ready to put their shoulder to the wheel.*

Thus, from a rough outline of a plan of campaign under four headings the fourth and least important is torn from its context, is made the central idea, and all the authority claimed for this one item that might be allowed to the mighty conception of which it formed comparatively a minor part. And this before any real study had been given to the plan. It may be here remarked, as far as the large conception was concerned, that when four months later the Expeditionary Force did land, they had no map of any value. The Staff Officer of the Commander-in-Chief, Sir Ian Hamilton, could not find out if there were any roads suitable for mechanical transport, or even any roads at all! The Expedition expected to find water: there was practically none.

The great consensus of opinion was against a purely naval attempt, because the chance of success in forcing the Dardanelles was small, and the effect of a hostile fleet appearing off Constantinople of very doubtful value. In its attempt to force the passage of the Straits would be fatal to it at all.

Mr. Churchill, however, chose to force it on, and in so doing seriously compromised the subsequent combined operation.

It would be as well to pause at this point to offer some remarks on the powers a First Lord legitimately possesses, on some of those that Mr. Churchill usurped, and on the personal relations that existed between him and the naval members of the Board and higher naval officers generally. The First Lord, by the Order in Council of 1869, is supreme in finance and administration. His colleagues on the Board advise and he decides. The Secretariat, the custodians of continuity and masters of precedent, combining with these their legitimate functions, the bureaucrat's love of power and dislike of responsibility, never lose an opportunity to emphasize the First Lord's authority under this order. The legality of the Order in Council is very questionable, its inexpediency in view of the danger of the appointment of such a First Lord as Mr. Churchill is unquestionable. To anyone of Mr. Churchill's temperament, the temptation to misuse his power was irresistible. His personality excited the antipathy of nearly every naval officer with whom he came in contact officially before the war. He is more American than English, and the English part of him is of a different variety from that which finds favour with the typical naval officer.

Now, when Mr. Churchill went to the Admiralty, he went convinced that he could teach the naval officer his business. He saw no necessity for treating with respect officers old enough to be his father and who had grown grey in the service. He did not appreciate the fact, a commonplace to those trained to responsibility, that a superior's first care is for the authority of his subordinates rather than for his own. He imagined that he was in supreme naval command, whereas under the Naval Discipline Act the First Lord has no personal authority to give a dog to run for him.

He undermined the discipline of the Service by the methods used in obtaining information on practices already forbidden. Two instances will suffice as illustrations:

Mr. Churchill was on one occasion shown round and visited a large private firm and inspected a new submarine completing. Her captain, a young man who had just received his first command, was led on to talk freely. Aspiring youth is always intolerant of age and experience, and no doubt this individual was naval enough to let it be known that he did not see eye to eye with his superiors. He was, however, flabbergasted on returning after all he had said in the form of a report to the First Lord and to find his protests over-ruled by a wholly wrongful assumption of an executive authority on the part of that statesman. On his return to the Admiralty, Mr. Churchill set up a committee consisting of the Third Sea Lord, the Commodore of Submarines, and others to consider and report to him on this most irregular appointment so improperly obtained, quite oblivious of the indignity inflicted on these highly placed officers. By obeying the First Lord this young officer had rendered himself liable to punishment by sentence of a court-martial. Had the ship been in commission the First Lord would have rendered himself liable.

In the second case the captain in charge of air units at a home port was summoned to a conference on board the *Enchantress*, to discover many of his subordinates there assembled without his knowledge or authority or that of his commander-in-chief. To his stupefaction he next discovered that Mr. Churchill was encouraging these subordinates to criticize and reflect upon their superiors, actually present. The upshot was that the commander-in-chief's remonstrance was couched in terms so uncomplimentary to the First Lord that the latter announced his intention of causing the commander-in-chief to strike his flag. This was too much for the Sea Lords, who in their turn intimated their intention to resign. Mr. Churchill felt fully equal to this contingency. Not so Mr. Asquith, the Prime Minister. This was too strong meat for him, not by any means a delicate feeder. And so the First Lord had to climb down and submit to the imposition of safeguards against the recurrence of such a lamentable episode. Mr. Churchill, however, was allowed to get even with the captain who had withstood him by paying off his ship recently fitted out for this particular service at great cost, and thus depriving him of his command under the guise of reorganization. In this case Mr. Churchill not only imperilled the officers he incited to insubordination, but rendered himself liable to arrest and trial.

Lord Fisher, when he left the Admiralty, by a masterstroke arranged for Sir Arthur Wilson to replace him—of enormous ability, unquestioned integrity, and venerated by the whole fleet, but of such a peculiarly self-centred temperament that it was obvious that the experiment could not in good faith and loyalty remain unaware of the immense powers of mischief there was to undo in naval administration and above all of discipline. Let it be said that he resigned there was to undo in naval of First Sea Lord under compulsion and against his own wishes.

This was the officer that Mr. Churchill met on appointment as First Lord, and whom, on finding him in his way, he incontinently dismissed, together with his naval colleagues, to replace him by an officer of a very different type. On November 16, 1911, Mr. Churchill wrote: "I pronounce decidedly in favour of Sir Francis Bridgeman as First Sea Lord. He is a fine sailor, with the full confidence of the Service afloat, and with the aptitude for working with, and through, a staff well developed. If, as would no doubt be the case, he should bring Captain de Bartolomé as his Naval Assistant, I am satisfied that the business of his office would proceed smoothly and with dispatch."

Sir Francis Bridgeman ultimately met the same fate as his predecessor. Captain de Bartolomé remained and subsequently became Naval Secretary to Mr. Churchill, which post he occupied during the progress of the Dardanelles campaign.

The effect on the Service of the dismissal of Sir Arthur Wilson and the whole of his naval colleagues except the Controller, soon to follow them, was severe.

It was difficult to accept an appointment at the hands of Mr. Churchill, remain in it at his sole pleasure, and at the same time retain a true degree of self-respect, the quality most essential to a naval commander, especially as it was openly stated that the First Lord in his selection attached more importance to a five minutes' interview than to the study of an officer's whole career and the opinions of his superiors and contemporaries.

As an illustration of Mr. Churchill's methods of patronage, the following may be quoted: An officer, after several years' experience of a special type of vessel, latterly at the Admiralty, asked to be considered for a command of a ship in that line. He was told that it depended on the personal pleasure of the First Lord, and accordingly solicited an interview. He replied that he had considered that while at the Admiralty an officer's qualifications were made known, and the intermediary remarked that "he did not fancy his chance."

The effect of Mr. Churchill's rule at the Admiralty can be best described by quoting extracts from the Report of the Dardanelles Commission:

*It is thus abundantly clear that, although no formal and official change was made, the spirit in which the business of the Admiralty was conducted underwent a great transformation immediately after the outbreak of the war. The Board of Admiralty sank into insignificance, its place being taken by the Staff Group. The Board was, even, to a less extent than previously, able to assume any "collective responsibility" for the general conduct of affairs. The individual members of the Board were not duly informed of passing events. They were not consulted before the naval attack on the Dardanelles was made. It is also clear that Mr. Churchill was informed as regards the condition under which Admiralty business was conducted when he stated to the Commission that the members of the War Council were entitled to assume "that any view laid before them by the First Lord of the Admiralty was the considered view of the naval authorities"...*

In the same document is quoted a statement handed in by Commodore Lambert, Fourth Sea Lord:

*On November 23, 1915, the Junior Sea Lords addressed collectively a minute to the present First Lord (Mr. Arthur Balfour), in which they said: "The conception of the status of a Member of the Board in Council that the supremacy of the First Lord is complete and unassailable, has been pushed too far, and has tended to influence such at some future time to the Imperial, national safety...."*

*"The present time may not be the proper one for effecting drastic changes, but of this we are certain—it is the proper and opportune moment to again call the attention of the First Lord to these matters and to express our conviction that had the naval members of the Board been regularly and collectively consulted on large questions of war policy during the progress of the present naval campaign, some of least of the events which the Empire does at this moment deplore so bitterly would not have happened, and that until the authority and responsibility of the Sea Lords is enlarged and defined, there will be no adequate assurance*

*that similar disasters will not recur in the future."*

This, then, was the statesman who, on his own initiative and responsibility, set going a naval attack without military support with a view to forcing the defences of the Dardanelles to an end which was to appear off Constantinople.

The action Mr. Churchill took was characteristic. The first step in an operation of this magnitude is usually the careful selection of the commander or commanders. As will be seen, Lord Fisher favoured Sir Doveton Sturdee. It is now generally known that the command was offered to him and by him refused, on the ground of the impracticability of the scheme. Sir Doveton Sturdee's career and his recent experience as Chief of Staff at the Admiralty rendered his opinion worthy of every respect. It was ignored.

Vice-Admiral Carden was in actual command in the Eastern Mediterranean. It does him no injustice to say that he did not possess Admiral Sturdee's qualifications for the task. He could have reached London in three days, but Mr. Churchill communicated with him by wire instead on January 3rd:

*FROM FIRST LORD:*

*Do you consider the forcing of the Dardanelles by ships alone a practical operation?*

*It is assumed that old battleships fitted with mine-bumpers would be used, preceded by colliers or other merchant craft as mine-bumpers or sweepers.*

*Importance of results would justify severe loss.*

*Let me know your views.*

On January 5th he received the reply:

*I do not consider Dardanelles can be rushed.*

*They might be forced by extended operations with large numbers of ships.*

On the same date Mr. Churchill asked Admiral Sir Henry Jackson to prepare a memorandum on the subject. Mr. Churchill records this memorandum on the 6th. Admiral Jackson was strongly opposed, and pointed out the probability of little result accruing, even if the passage was made successfully. He was ignored.

On January 6th, but before the receipt of the before-mentioned Memorandum, the First Lord sent a further telegram:

Your view is agreed with by high authorities here. Please telegraph in detail what you think could be done by extended operations, what force would be needed, and how you consider it should be used.

This was not fair to Admiral Carden. It misled him into believing that the high authorities were other than they were. Lord Fisher had not seen the telegram. It opened up a prospect of a large operation, the means for the carrying out of which, if they existed at all, were in England, as also was the latest intelligence, and the knowledge of the state of affairs in other theatres of war, all of which had a bearing on the proposed operations.

The Board of Admiralty was not consulted, and thus the knowledge, experience, and information to be found there, and essential to the success of the operations, was robbed of the project.

Mr. Churchill says:

*On January 11th arrived the detailed Carden plan. It was in its details largely the work of a very able officer of Marines—Captain Godfrey (who was at that time Admiral's Staff)—and of the gunnery experts of the* Inflexible

It is not necessary to quote it. Mr. Churchill says: "This plan produced a great impression on everyone who saw it."

It should have caused the very greatest disquietude. That the details should be worked out by a captain of marines was presented to Mr. Churchill, but it should not have met with the approbation of Admirals. It contained the germ of the fatal feature which distinguished this operation—the failure to appreciate the strength of the current running through the Dardanelles and its effect on the operation of mine-sweeping, and that it was the minefield with the guns and searchlights protecting it, and not the forts, that was the principal obstacle to the passage of the Dardanelles. Twelve mine-sweepers were asked for, including "perhaps four fleet-sweepers." There could be no "perhaps" in the matter of fleet-sweepers, which means fast steamers of light draught. It was idle to think of this matter without a large flotilla of them, and this was eventually represented to the Vice-Admiral when the operation, which took place on March 18th, was under discussion at a Council of War. The

Admiral's reply was that they had been asked for and the Admiralty had replied they were not available. Mr. Churchill now issues his orders:

*Secretary,*

*First Sea Lord, Chief of Staff.*

*January 12th.*

*I. The forcing of the Dardanelles as proposed, and the arrival of a squadron strong enough to defeat the Turkish Fleet in the Sea of Marmora, would be a victory of first importance and change to our advantage the whole situation of the war in the East.*

*II. It would appear possible to provide the forces required by Admiral Carden without weakening the margin necessary in home waters as follows:*

*(He names battleships and battle-cruisers).*

*III. The above takes no account of four French battleships on the spot, and six others reported available. . . .*

*IV. Operations could begin on February 1st, by long-range fire, from* Queen Elizabeth *on forts at the entrance. It is not necessary to develop the full attack until the effect of the first stage of the operation has become apparent. All arrangements should be secretly concerted for carrying the plan through, the seaplanes and ancillary craft being supplied—Admiral Carden being consulted. Definite plans should be worked out accordingly.*

*W. S. C.*

He adds quaintly enough that Lord Fisher approved this Minute, which was addressed to him as an order. Having thus contrived to start the undertaking on bad lines, Mr. Churchill, in complete ignorance of the realities of the problem, proceeds to take a leading part in a spirited controversy on the relative merits of ships and forts. He leads his reader in his book into a maze of technicalities as he appears to have done his colleagues in the Cabinet. Any record of the opinion of the Director of Naval Ordnance is conspicuous by its absence. However, out of all the medley there is one plum which should not be missed:

*All these old ships were doomed to be scrapped in 1915. Their crews were needed to man the great fleets and to commission of new ships which were now coming into the water and requiring to be commissioned. All the "Majestics," all the "Canopuses," all the "Formidables," all the "Duncans" were inexorably marked for final extinction within the next year or fifteen months.*

Mr. Churchill has never explained how, when considerable losses had been suffered in the minefields and Narrows under a heavy fire, the crews of the sinking ships could be saved "to man the great fleets and flotillas of new ships." He next, on January 13th, explains matters to the War Council. His principal theme is the reduction of the forts and he adds: "Once the forts were reduced the minefields could be cleared." This shows how little he understood the problem, for it was impossible to reduce the forts until the minefields had been at least partly cleared, and no means had been provided for sweeping the mine-fields.

No wonder this sapient exposition of the problem produced that remarkable order from the War Council, for ever a monument to their wisdom and knowledge. It is dated January 13th:

*That the Admiralty should also prepare for a naval expedition in February to bombard and take the Gallipoli Peninsula with Constantinople as its objective.*

The Royal Commission states:

*It is impossible to read all the evidence, or to study the voluminous papers which have been submitted to us, without being struck with the atmosphere of vagueness and want of precision which seems to have characterized the proceedings of the War Council. We have already (par. 28) mentioned that some of those present at the meetings of the Council left without having any very clear idea of what had or had not been decided. The decision of the Council, taken on January 13th, is another case in point. The Admiralty was to "prepare" for a naval expedition, and to prepare it "complete," and after the Admiralty plan was matured, actual approval of the bombardment was withheld.*

Lord Fisher now became reluctant to the verge of resignation. He did not think that the attempt to get through by the Fleet alone "was a feasible operation." He thought "it was a mad thing to do." Sir Arthur Wilson did not see any harm in it so long as the operation could be stopped, if necessary, before the Government became too deeply committed. Sir Henry Oliver and Captain de

Bartolomé would have preferred a combined operation but acquiesced.

The Royal Commission's report contains the following:

*We should here mention that at a somewhat late stage of our inquiry Sir George Arthur intimated to us that he was in a position to give information bearing upon the question of the extent to which Lord Kitchener was primarily responsible for the initiation of the Dardanelles expedition. He subsequently handed in a statement descriptive of a conversation which he had had with Lord Kitchener, and which was to the following effect:*

*Lord Kitchener stated that "at a conference to which he was invited by the First Lord of the Admiralty, when the passage of the Dardanelles was the subject of discussion, he protested vigorously against any such an undertaking by the Navy without very strong and very carefully prepared support from and co-operation with the Army"; that the First Lord had stated that the experience of the past was no longer admissible by reason of the "marvellous potentialities of the* Queen Elizabeth,*" which ship was about to be sent to the Dardanelles; that Lord Kitchener admitted that "he had no expert knowledge of the* Queen Elizabeth *and was therefore not in a position to contradict or depreciate the statements as to her astounding effectiveness, which the First Lord had alleged would revolutionize all previous estimates of naval warfare"; and that he had "contented himself with renewing his protest in which he was sure that he voiced all military opinion; but he said that his inevitable uneasiness would have been considerably dimished had he been able to satisfy himself that the First Lord's confidence both in the* Queen Elizabeth *and in the success of his plan was wholly and wholeheartedly shared by his naval advisers."*

*Much depends upon the date upon which this conversation occurred. Sir George Arthur was unable to give a precise date, but it resulted from the examination that without any doubt it was held about the same time as the War Council which took place on May 14th. At that Council, indeed, Lord Kitchener expressed himself in terms somewhat similar to those used by Sir George Arthur. He read the following statement:*

*When the Admiralty proposed to force the passage of the Dardanelles by means of the Fleet alone, I doubted whether the attempt would succeed, but was led to believe it was possible by the First Lord's statements of the power of the* Queen Elizabeth *and the Admiralty Staff paper showing how the operation was to be conducted ... I regret that I was led to agree in the entreprise by the statements made, particularly as to the power of the* Queen Elizabeth, *of which I had no means of judging.*

*It will be seen therefore, that Sir George Arthur's evidence has no direct bearing upon the immediate subject of our inquiry, namely, the opinions Lord Kitchener expressed during the period of origin and inception, which, as we have already mentioned (par. 2) we consider to have closed on March 23, 1915.*

As the *Queen Elizabeth* was about to be sent to the Dardanelles, the conference of Lord Kitchener with the First Lord must have taken place not later than the end of January or beginning of February. The conclusion as to the relevancy is therefore a little difficult to understand.

The Royal Commission states that

> *Looking to all the facts of the case, we are disposed to think that undue importance was attached to the ease with which the Belgian forts were destroyed, and that the extent to which there was any analogy between those forts and the forts at the Dardanelles was overrated.*

It is by no means clear that either the Director of Naval Ordinance or the Third Sea Lord were among those who fell into the error referred to. Indeed, had they been consulted, they, in all probability, would have made clear the difference between an attack by large-capacity high-explosive shells from 16-inch high-angle siege guns on cupola forts with heavy shield over the guns, which shields were a target instead of a protection, and the attack from the sea with 15-inch powder-filled common shell fired at a low trajectory at unshielded guns in an open emplacement.

It should not either have been necessary to send the seaplanes out to the Dardanelles to find out that they could rarely find water smooth enough to rise from into the air, and when up that their engine-power was insufficient to take them over the forts at the Narrows at the requisite height. The *Queen Elizabeth* depended on these planes for observation of her fire across the Peninsula.

On such slender grounds did Mr. Churchill assure Lord Kitchener that

the experience of the past was no longer admissible by reason of the marvellous potentialities of the Queen Elizabeth.

Mr. Churchill, discussing the plan so far, contends that the genesis of this plan and its elaboration were purely naval and professional in their character:

*It was Vice-Admiral Carden and his Staff gunnery officers who proposed the gradual method of piecemeal reduction by long-range bombardment. It was Admiral Jackson and the Admiralty Staff which examined the plan and studied and approved its details. Right or wrong, it was a Service plan!*

Mr. Churchill starts as the War Lord giving his orders to his inferiors. The staff gives advice to these orders without prejudice, and either without comment or with criticisms.

When the orders are called in question, Mr. Churchill becomes the civilian, without technical knowledge, and the orders are the orders of the staff, and not his,—oh no!

Had the Sea Lords and Naval officers and departments they supervised been asked to advise, the problem involved in the forcing of the Dardanelles would have been properly appreciated, and, more especially so, if the step, obviously dictated by common prudence, of establishing personal communication between the scene of operations and the Admiralty, had been adopted.

The Royal Commission found that the First Lord and not Lord Kitchener was responsible for the attempt to force the Straits by ships alone.

Mr. Churchill chose to regard the War Council's minute of January 13th as a mandate and pressed on.

To force the Dardanelles it was first necessary to destroy the forts at the entrance, clear that entrance and the lower reaches of the Straits of mines, thus enabling ships to enter and bombard. This operation was carried out with ease and practically without loss. A wholly false impression was created in the mind of Mr. Churchill. Had he read the Naval Intelligence Handbook, he would have seen that these forts were badly placed and were bound to fall to naval attack. As targets alone they were as easy as those at the Narrows were difficult. They were unsupported, and ships could anchor out of range and fire at them at leisure in fine weather. Instead, he concluded that the forts at the Narrows would be reduced with the same ease.

The Fleet could now enter. The *Queen Elizabeth, Inflexible, Lord Nelson*, and *Agamemnon* could bombard the forts at the Narrows out of range of the latter. They could not anchor on account of the fire of the howitzers and guns in concealed positions, and of the fire of the four advanced forts. The older ships, bombarding them at extreme range, came not only under the fire experienced by the more modern ships, but of that of some of the forts at the Narrows. The available sweepers could keep the necessary range for this long-range bombardment clear if the Turks did not show too much enterprise in mine-laying at night. This they were probably not in a position to do owing to the lack of the necessary mines. To destroy the forts it was necessary to approach as near as possible.

Now, if a sufficient number of fast sweepers had been on the spot, it might have been possible to sweep some of the ships up to within destructive range whilst others kept down the fire of the forts, the sweepers' numbers and speed making it possible for them to push on. This might have done something to counter and disconcert; while other sweepers were held in reserve ready to take the place of those sunk or disabled.

The mine-sweepers actually sent out were trawlers, of such deep draught that they could themselves strike mines, and of such small speed that they could not sweep against the current, even in the places where it was not at its strongest. The number sent was inadequate in any case. It was therefore necessary that, under a concentration fire throughout, they should steam slowly against the current until they reached the desired spot, get out their sweeps there—an operation requiring time—and then sweep down. This was found to be beyond the endurance of the fishermen who constituted their crews, as might have been expected, and when these were replaced by naval crews it was discovered to be impossible by day. At night, the blinding effect of the searchlights, the casualties to men and mines caused by the heavy fire, and the nerve strain imposed were such as to render the sweep of little value in removing mines; and had the attempts been continued the small sweeping flotilla would have soon ceased to exist without having made any permanent impression on the mine-field for the mines swept could be replaced by night.

When the Russians had no rifles they armed their troops with clubs for action which they could not avoid, but they did not seek the enemy so armed. Had Mr. Churchill allowed the proper organization of the Admiralty to work, or had he established personal communication between the Fleet and the Admiralty, all this, obvious to those on the spot, must have been foreseen, and this ill-starred attempt would never have taken place. There were military officers who knew every inch of the Peninsula; they were never sent for. There were people who had spent their lives in these waters, and could have told the Government that no military operations involving landing on open beaches was possible before the end of April. They were not consulted.

The possibility of military support now opens up.

Having started the naval operations on thoroughly unsound lines, Mr. Churchill makes an appreciation on the military situation without the first requisites—correct maps and adequate information of the enemy's forces.

It has only to go on with Mr. Churchill's book to find a complete failure to understand the situation at every point:

*Page 211—The increasing perplexities of the naval attack and the surprising ease with which the small party of marines had been landed at the entrance on the 4th of February, made the immediate employment of troops very tempting, both at the Admiralty and on the spot.*

And again, page 205:

*Landing parties sent ashore on March 4th met with much stiffer resistance difficult to reach the forts.*

Now for the facts. The parties first referred to were landed from battleships on patrol at the entrance to the Straits in February. The Turks did not keep their troops uselessly manning the trenches on the coast in the severe weather then mostly prevailing, but at the village of Krithia, some few miles inland, or at some intermediate spot. On the Asiatic shore also the troops were not stationed actually on the coast. When the landing parties went ashore the Turks started to meet them, but always arrived too late to oppose the actual landing and were held back by fire from the ships. There were three separate landings at Seddel Bahr and two at Kum Kale. On March 4th the companies of the Naval Division could be descried, a serried khaki mass, on the decks of destroyers approaching from the south, more than half an hour before they arrived at the shore to receive them on landing. There was nothing in the circumstances of these various landings to give any indication of the numbers of enemy troops in these areas.

*Page 213—It seems probable that if the 29th Division had been on the spot in fighting order it could have been landed with whatever troops were sent from Egypt at this period without severe loss and could have occupied very important and probably decisive positions.*

Heavy guns and howitzers, including our new 15-inch howitzer, could also have been landed and brought into action.

As to landing troops in numbers earlier, *the weather absolutely forbade it even a day earlier than that on which it took place, April 25th.* The landing-places would have been wrecked by the heavy seas beating on them, and all communications stopped for days. Any movement of the 29th Division would, moreover, have been met by a counter move by the Turks. The actual landing of this Division was opposed by three companies only, with one in reserve. The terrible losses inflicted by this small number on our troops are well known.

A 15-inch howitzer eventually arrived at Mudros. It was *never possible to land* it on the Peninsula owing to lack of facilities for dealing with such heavy weights.

So much for criticisms based on an authority on combined operations; the purpose of this paper is, however, concerned with his project for forcing the Dardanelles by naval means unaided.

Mr. Churchill, on page 214 of his book, tells us:

*The original Carden plan of gradual piecemeal reduction has been pursued. It has not failed, but it has lagged, and it is now so feebly pressed as almost to be at a standstill.*

And on page 205 we are told:

*The mine-sweeping trawlers which have been provided for this service proved inadequate for such a service.*

Again, on page 208, we find:

*During these days I began to doubt whether there was sufficient determination behind the attack. In one of his telegrams, for instance, the Admiral reported that the mine-sweepers had been driven back by heavy fire, which, he added, caused no casualties. Considering what was happening on the Western Front and the desperate tasks and fearful losses which were accepted almost daily by the Allied troops, I could not but feel disquieted by an opinion of this kind.*

If the Admiral were to accept the losses and sweep a small portion of the mine-field, what was he to do next? Without replacement of sweepers he could not continue, and a check in an operation of this nature meant beginning all over again when reinforcements arrived.

On March 11th, having informed the Admiral that no fast sweepers were available, and being still apparently unaware of the strength of the current, as described in the Sailing Directions, the First Lord wired to Admiral Carden:

*We suggest for your consideration a point has now been reached when it is necessary, choosing favourable weather conditions, to overwhelm the forts at the Narrows at decisive range. Under cover of the fire the guns of the forts might be destroyed by landing parties and as much as possible of the mine-fields swept up. This operation might have to be continued until all the forts of the Narrows have been destroyed and the approaches cleared of mines.*

Admiral Carden must, by this time, have already been a sick man or unduly influenced, for we find him under date of 15th replying:

*I fully appreciate the situation and intend, as stated in my telegram of March 14th, to vigorously attack fortresses of the Narrows, clearing mine-fields under cover of attack.*

Let us consider for a moment what this attack meant. Ships had hitherto engaged these forts at long range, just within the reach of the guns of the forts at maximum elevation. As they drew nearer the accuracy of the fire from both sides would have increased. Ships would be plunging fire, their horizontal armour being weak, and ships when under water close alongside have a counter-mining effect.

As the sweeping operations progressed, the farther up sweepers got the greater their difficulties would have become, on account of the increased strength of the current, the greater intensity of fire, and the losses they must have sustained without replacement. In the very limited area thus swept, battleships would have had to manoeuvre, liable to be put out of control at any moment by a lucky shot and perhaps caused to drift out of the swept track, to be hit by one or more mines, or even to hit a mine in that area, for the

sweeping could not be thorough. A ship mined under these circumstances would most probably be lost by capsizing after a short
interval. The auxiliaries would render no aid in saving life without
abandoning sweeping operations, which would be inadmissible.
The plan was preposterous, even with a force of fast mine-sweepers,
three or four times the number, which would be employed at one
time.

Now we come to the events of March 18, 1915.

The preliminary bombardment had taken place. The second
British squadron had replaced the French, who had retired with the
loss of the *Bouvet*, sunk by a mine which exploded a magazine. The
second squadron, after bombardment, had been ordered to draw
back out of range, the mine-sweeping trawlers had slowly made
their way to a position between the ships of this inshore squadron, preparatory to sweeping in front of them, when a burst of fire
from the shore fell on them of such intensity that they all put their
helms over and fled from it.

As they made their way out with the current, orders were given
to the captain in charge of destroyers to endeavour to rally them,
but some hours must have elapsed before they could regain the
position they had left. Nothing more could be done until the
sweepers returned and got to work. Thus the total inadequacy of
the arrangements made for clearing the mines, sufficiently obvious
before to those on the spot, should have become evident even to
Mr. Churchill.

On page 215, Mr. Churchill says:

*The prolonged bombardment of the Dardanelles had assuredly drawn
continually increasing Turkish forces to the Gallipoli Peninsula and
the Asiatic shore; guns, ammunition, and material had been collected;
the Turks were so ill-provided,"[1] had been scraped and dragged from
every point or were on the move.*

*Moreover, the Russians had by a brilliant effort largely restored the
situation in the Caucasus . . . but now it was certainly an arguable policy to close the account. . . so far from wishing to break off the operation
the First Sea Lord was never at any time now so resolute in its support.
Sir A. Wilson, Sir H. Jackson, Admiral Oliver, Commodore de Bar-*

1     It was our artillery, not the Turks', that later received the nick-
name of "quick-firers." Guns had been moved from one place to another,
however, allowance being only one round per gun.

*tolomé, all were united and agreed to press on, and press hard.*

Amazing, if true.

Mr. Churchill, however, misses the point, which he unconsciously establishes in the first paragraph quoted above, that this naval attack, which was bound to fail, had an effect disastrous to the military expedition that was to follow.

On March 18th, three battleships had been sunk and a battle-cruiser disabled by mines. Two French battleships *Gaulois* and *Suffren* had been so severely damaged by shell-fire as to be in danger of sinking. Subsequently the *Triumph*, *Majestic*, and *Goliath* were sunk by torpedoes with great loss of life in the last two cases, and yet, from start to finish, Mr. Churchill advocated an assault on the forts of the Narrows through extensive mine-fields, by ships very vulnerable to under-water attack by mine, torpedo, or shell, and by mine-fields without the means to deal with the mines.

In their conclusions on page 41 of their Report the Royal Commission finds that:

*Mr. Churchill appears to have advocated the attack by ships alone before the War Council on a certain amount of half-hearted and hesitating expert opinion which favoured a tentative or progressive scheme, beginning with an attack upon the outer forts. This attack, if successful, was to be followed by further operations against the main defences of the Narrows. There does not appear to have been direct support or direct opposition to this course by the responsible naval and military advisers, Lord Fisher and Sir James Wolfe Murray, as to the practicability of carrying out the operation as approved by the War Council, viz: "To bombard and take the Gallipoli Peninsula, with Constantinople as its objective."*

Had the Navy been more strongly represented on this Commission, it is conceivable they would have dealt with the First Lord less gently.

The danger of a continuance of the unrestricted authority of the First Lord should be realized. It rests not on an Act of Parliament but on an Order in Council, that is, the autocratic order of the Government, and of very doubtful legality. It has been shown how, in the case of an individual like Mr. Churchill, it can lead to an assumption of authority in matters naval which he has no qualifications to fulfil.

When Mr. Asquith appointed Mr. Churchill to the Admiralty, he may have done so in ignorance of the extent of the authority of the First Lord, for at the War Council he assumed that he spoke in the name of the Board. He had, however, no excuse for not knowing the man he was dealing with. He knew Mr. Churchill had dismissed a whole Naval Board (the Controller excepted, but not for long); he himself was a party to this. He must have known that Sir Francis Bridgeman (Mr. Churchill's own choice, under the conditions cited) was also dismissed, though Mr. Churchill alleges ill-health as the reason for his departure. Mr. Asquith had to refuse peremptorily the First Lord's application for a commission as Lieutenant-General to Command at Antwerp—a suggestion in itself sufficient to show the irresponsibility of the applicant.

Now, the danger of naval or military control by a politician lies in this: Politics are pursued in an atmosphere of unreality. They deal not with actualities but with semblances of things. The more democratic the institutions, the less real politics become. The House of Commons contains an ever-increasing number of barristers whose business it is to speak to a brief rather than on the merits of the case. Members gain in power and influence in proportion to their powers of misrepresentation, most notable in the case of Labour leaders.

To many of these men, the practical man and the man of conscience and rectitude is anathema. Hence politicians like Mr. Churchill advance military men whose brethren would not always or even often choose to lead them in war. Courtesy is necessary to a nature like Mr. Churchill's. The best naval officer is inapt in the art.

War is the opposite to politics. It is as realistic as the other is fantastic. The shell, the torpedo, and the mine will not be ignored, nor can they be rendered innocuous like a parliamentary opposition by an ingenious grouping of words.

Mr. Churchill had a prepossession, verging on mania—the forcing of the Dardanelles and the capture of Constantinople. He did not know what this involved. How should he? He did not choose to find out. Men have met a disgraceful death for less! He thought to replace all the necessary knowledge, experience, and study by an enormous, scarcely sane, faith in his own magnetic influence learnt from London. He used the autocratic power he possessed at the Admiralty to set aside those who stood in his way: he used his eloquence and hypnotic skill to set aside the scruples of his colleagues.

If the selected Admiral, who knew his Churchill, declined, he chose the man to hand, and by the politician's acts against which the Admiral has been rendered helpless and is now helpless, made him into a puppet. With that damnable ingeniousness he possesses he made his way through all opposition until he attained his end, and when the inevitable failures attended his efforts, the same lamentable qualities are shown in the endeavour to absolve himself from blame by the aspersion of the characters alike of his victims and of his tools.

The Expedition of the Dardanelles was redeemed from being an utter act of folly by the great qualities displayed by the King's forces and those of the French Republic. Leadership was entirely absent at home, thanks principally to Mr. Churchill, and after him to Mr. Asquith, who put him at the Admiralty and kept him there. The leadership at the front was what might have been expected under the lamentable circumstances.

Mr. Churchill owes his immunity to two things—the doing away with the court-martial which should follow the loss of a ship or ships (this was his own act), and the usurpation of recent years by the Board of Admiralty, which means the First Lord, of the right to deny a trial. This was exercised by Mr. McKenna when the late Lord Beresford desired to bring a subordinate flag officer to trial, because the prosecution of that officer would have resulted in the exposure of the Admiralty.

Similarly, had the Admiral and General in command at the Dardanelles been brought to trial, the actions of Mr. Churchill and Lord Kitchener would have been investigated, though indirectly, by competent tribunals—and the Admiral at least could not have been left so exposed to the innuendo of Mr. Churchill.

There can be little doubt that in such event Mr. Churchill would have been effectively silenced and his book, *The World Crisis*, would never have appeared. The right of an individual to demand trial should therefore be restored, as also the right of any superior to insist on the trial of his subordinate on sufficient grounds shown. There is also urgent need for a disciplinary code and tribunal for the members of the Permanent Civil Service.

Lastly, there is even greater need for a court before which the actions of Ministers can be brought in question. Impeachment has fallen into desuetude; something else must replace it in the interests of the national safety.

During the war it was said of Mr. Churchill: "Winston does not read history, he makes it." What of the history he made at the Dardanelles?

**FLAG OFFICER**

Explicit iste liber, scriptor sit crimine
liber, Christus scriptorem custodiat ac
det honorem

Ὥσπερ ξένοι χαίρουσιν ἰδεῖν
πατρίδα, οὕτως καὶ οἱ γράφοντες
ἰδεῖν βιβλίου τέλος

श्रीकृष्णार्पणमस्तु

書成矣，感盡天地

סלוע ארוב לאל חבש סלשנו סת

"of making many books there
is no end; and much study is a
weariness of the flesh"
- Ecclesiastes 12:12

BULKINGTON BOOKS

www.ingramcontent.com/pod-product-compliance
Lightning Source LLC
Chambersburg PA
CBHW071152120626
46546CB00006B/2238